One Big Happy Family

Also by Lisa Rogak

Dan Brown: The Unauthorized Biography

Dogs of Courage: The Heroism and Heart of Working Dogs Around the World

The Dogs of War: The Courage, Love, and Loyalty of Military Working Dogs

And Nothing but the Truthiness: The Rise (and Further Rise) of Stephen Colbert

Michelle Obama in Her Own Words: The Views and Values of America's First Lady

Barack Obama in His Own Words

Haunted Heart: The Life and Times of Stephen King

A Boy Named Shel: The Life and Times of Shel Silverstein

One Big Happy Family

Heartwarming Stories of Animals Caring for One Another

LISA ROGAK

THOMAS DUNNE BOOKS

ST. MARTIN'S GRIFFIN

NEW YORK

11/13

THOMAS DUNNE BOOKS.

An imprint of St. Martin's Press.

ONE BIG HAPPY FAMILY. Copyright © 2013 by Lisa Rogak. All rights reserved. Printed in the United States of America. For information, address St. Martin's Press, 175 Fifth Avenue, New York, N.Y. 10010.

www.thomasdunnebooks.com

...tins.com

9781250035400

ISBN   ack)

St. Martin's Griffin books may be purchased for educational, business, or promotional use. For information on bulk purchases, please contact Macmillan Corporate and Premium Sales Department at 1-800-221-7945 extension 5442 or write specialmarkets@macmillan.com.

First Edition: October 2013

10 9 8 7 6 5 4 3 2

For Alex, because we're a bit of an odd mix ourselves …

Contents

One Big Happy Family

Introduction

Koko is a female gorilla who uses sign language to communicate with the humans who care for her at the Gorilla Foundation in Woodside, California. In addition to knowing approximately one thousand signs in American Sign Language, she can understand more than two thousand spoken English words. In 1984, she asked for — and received — a small kitten she could care for. Her human companions watched in awe as Koko treated the kitten — who she had named All Ball — as tenderly as if she was her own offspring. When All Ball was killed by a car, Koko painfully grieved at her premature loss, signing "Bad, sad, bad" and "Frown, cry, frown, sad."

Almost everyone has heard about the story of Koko the gorilla and her kitten, but there are countless other heartwarming stories to be found. They exemplify not only the best of what animals can accomplish, but also serve as a stellar example of the caring and compassion that we humans can strive for. These rare and touching relationships prove beyond a shadow of a doubt that this instinct to love and nurture is real and, in some extraordinary cases, extends beyond the boundaries of species.

Indeed, everyone can identify with the feelings Koko experienced and spelled out. And, in fact, many other animals would, too. Koko presents only the tip of the iceberg when it comes to the incredible relationships and bonds of interspecies parenting. A new story seems to appear in the news and online every week, and more often than not, immediately goes viral.

"It's not unusual for animals to be nurturing toward any species," says John C. Wright, Ph.D., author of *Ain't Misbehavin': The Groundbreaking Program for Happy, Well-Behaved Pets and Their People,* and a certified applied animal behaviorist and professor of psychology at Mercer University. "The instinct to care for another animal can be hormonal, or simply related to age. If they're young, their behavior is malleable, and they're open to just about any experience, opportunity or companion. Like humans, animals, for the most part, yearn for company."[1]

For other animals, particularly birds, the drive to nurture and raise young is particularly acute, on both ends, for the parent and for the child. At the same time, however, it's deep within a newly hatched bird's genes to instantly connect with the first thing it sees when it opens its eyes, whether that be animal, vegetable, or mineral.

Imprinting is a phenomenon among geese, turkeys, and ducks that noted Austrian naturalist Konrad Lorenz studied and earmarked in the beginning of the twentieth century. According to Lorenz, these birds are preprogrammed to consider the first large-moving object they see in the first few critical hours and days after being hatched as their primary parent figure. Though you'll discover that cats, dogs, and birds of other species can serve as the parental stand-in, Lorenz also found that newly hatched birds can become attached to boots, balls, and in one instance, even electric trains.

"If you put an egg under a bird and if its instinct is strong enough it will go for it," said Graham Appleton of the British Trust for Ornithology. "For the chick, anything that is there at the time becomes the mother and it will make all the right noises to try and get food. The parent's instinct will be to feed the newborn.

"The little gosling's instinct will be to follow the parent around and copy whatever they do," he continued, describing one case when a peacock adopted a gosling. "This is certainly a strange situation and it may be a little confusing for the little bird. It will have some instinct of its own but it will be fascinating to see if it learns things like how to swim, which is something a peacock can't do."[2]

Based on the real-world experience of zoologists and staffers at wildlife sanctuaries and other rehabilitation centers around the world, interspecies-parenting cases tend to appear more frequently among animals — endangered or otherwise — in captivity than in the wild. In the case of orangutans and other primates in captivity (given efforts to save these endangered species and provide educational examples to the public), the living conditions for these animals are wildly different from the natural habitat they are accustomed to. So it naturally follows that their parenting styles and abilities would vary as well.

"Although we had endeavored to give our orangs the very best accommodation, we still could not reproduce the conditions they would have known in the wild," said the late Molly Badham, a founder of Twycross Zoo in Leicestershire, Great Britain. "In their natural environment, the males live alone, only joining the females for mating, and orang females with infants often travel with other such females in a kind of nursery group,"[3] an environment where the new mothers learn from more experienced veterans and come to know what to expect. In captivity, by contrast, males and females typically live together, which makes it possible for the number of births to be as frequent as once a year as the length of pregnancy mirrors that of a human.

Therefore, it's important that the human caretakers of these animals keep careful watch and know when it's time to step in and offer assistance in order to accommodate these differences. Happily, there's a virtual abundance of other animals that are eager to step in and assume the role of nursemaid, teacher, babysitter, or merely assist their humans wherever they need help. Molly Badham, for one, preferred dogs, particularly Great Danes, to serve as surrogate mothers and fathers for the chimps, orangutans, monkeys, and other primates that were often rejected by their mothers. "We found willing foster parents in our Great Danes, who were very tolerant of all the orphans who invaded their territory," said Badham. "Perhaps it was because all of the dogs were rescued and this background might have given them an affinity to other animals that were in need of help," she said.[4]

However, not only dogs prove to be adept at caring for orphaned animal babies. In the pages of *One Big Happy Family*, you will read about some pretty incredible combinations, from a peacock hatching and caring for a gosling to a pig helping to raise — and nurse — a kitten. But by far, the majority of stories involve a male or female dog acting as surrogate and foster parent. While some may wonder why this is so — perhaps it's attributable to the fact that dogs are the most common household pet — the truth is more prosaic: It comes down to breeding and the millennia of training that have made canines human's best friends as well as able to perform a wide variety of jobs according to a specific breed.

"Dogs have been genetically modified by us to be extremely sociable and extremely accepting," says Stanley Coren, Ph.D., professor of psychology at the University of British Columbia and author of numerous books about dogs, including *The Intelligence of Dogs: A Guide to the Thoughts, Emotions, and Inner Lives of Our Canine Companions*. "Generally speaking, the issue is something we call *neotony*, which simply refers to the fact that we have bred our dogs so that they are effectively puppies for their entire lives."[5]

Interestingly, as Coren points out, those canine breeds with more puppy-like physical characteristics, including larger ears that point downward and big eyes — and with fewer resemblances to wolves, such as eyes that are narrow and ears that point toward the sky — are more likely to serve as a surrogate parent to an animal of a different species.

"When these things happen with the less neotonized dogs, it will usually be an association involving a very young animal," says Coren. "Part of the reason for this is that very young mammals have pheromones that give them a characteristic 'baby smell.' One of the purposes of these pheromones is to excite protective instincts, or at least non-hostile instincts, in its own species. However, because of the similarity amongst all the mammals, we tend to find that other animals will respond to it."[6]

Some of the parent-child relationships you'll read about last for the lifetime of each animal, as in the case of the pig and the kitten; while some encounters last far less than that, as you'll discover with the story of the lioness and the baby antelope. Of course, since the lifespan of most animals is much shorter than ours, their childhood can sometimes be measured in weeks and months, instead of years. It's much more common for the adult animals to help do whatever it takes to bring the young one back from the brink of death, stick around for awhile to make sure the youngster can fly under his own power, and then step away so the young one can live the life that nature intended; in many cases, the goal is to help return the young to the wild.

The most important thing to realize is that in many cases, the animals you'll read about in *One Big Happy Family* went against type: Their parenting instincts defied their natural predator instincts where an encounter would typically result in injury and often death. The simple truth is that the siren call of their maternal or paternal drive was stronger.

Each acted as a parent to a baby animal desperately in need of one, and in doing so they serve as an inspiration to humans, parents or otherwise.

The Greyhound and Her Fawn, Her Fox Kits, Her Bunnies, and . . .

For some animals, their maternal — and paternal — instincts don't just stop at helping to raise one critter of another species. Some enjoy it so much — and indeed are so well-suited to the task — that they do so many times over.

In 2003, local police had found a young greyhound locked in a garden shed. It was clear she had been there for more than a few days because she was in pretty rough shape: She showed signs of having been abused before she was abandoned, and she was malnourished and covered with dirt. The police contacted Geoff Grewcock, who had founded the Nuneaton & Warwickshire Wildlife Sanctuary in Great Britain two years earlier, and he took her in to live among other abandoned and abused animals.

Originally, his goal was to bring the dog (christened Jasmine by the sanctuary) back to health, help her renew her trust of humans, and then find a new home for her, but then some-

Family Fact: Due to their unique structure, a greyhound's legs are too long and muscular to allow them to be able to sit.

thing unusual and heartwarming happened. As soon as Jasmine started to regain her health, she would accompany Grewcock around the grounds of the sanctuary, and took a great interest whenever a new animal arrived at the sanctuary, especially the very youngest ones. In essence, caring for these babies became Jasmine's job, and over the years, she served as surrogate mother to a variety of fox and badger cubs, chicks, guinea pigs, and rabbits.

The story of a young fawn's arrival at the sanctuary was typical of Jasmine's nurturing instincts. A neighbor found the fawn roaming in a field not far from the sanctuary's grounds. She was acting disoriented, and most likely her mother had been killed, so she was brought to the sanctuary. Grewcock named the fawn Bramble, and soon after her arrival, Jasmine greeted the scared fawn and promptly assumed responsibility for her care.

"They are inseparable," said Grewcock. "Bramble walks between her legs as they walk together round the sanctuary, and they keep kissing each other. It's absolutely marvelous. It's a real treat to see them."

He added that Jasmine treated every baby animal in the same way regardless of the species or breed: with lots of love and affection. Grewcock said he particularly marveled at how Jasmine interacted with the bunnies that came into the sanctuary, since greyhounds were bred to chase them. She even calmly sat while birds perched on her nose. "It is quite amazing, particularly as she is a greyhound breed and they are usually quite aggressive, which is why they're used for racing," he said. "She simply dotes on the animals as if they were her own, it's incredible to see."[1]

It's clear that Jasmine helped the new young arrivals in a number of ways: She made them feel more comfortable and eased the tension they felt in the wake of their abuse and/or abandonment, as well as helped them grow accustomed to their new home at the sanctuary. It didn't take long for the animals in her charge to feel close to her and cuddle and trust in her, and by extension to Grewcock and the other humans at the sanctuary.

Sadly, Jasmine passed away in 2011, but the inspiring story of her mothering instincts will live on.

The Hen and Her Ducklings

We all get confused from time to time. For example, when we fully intend to order a Diet Coke, we somehow end up with a chocolate milkshake. Occasionally, animals also get their wires crossed, with wonderfully charming results.

Take the case of Hilda the hen, who lived on a farm near Poole in Dorset, Great Britain. When she started sitting on a nest of five eggs in the spring of 2012, her owner, Philip

Palmer, fully expected to be greeted with a clutch of fluffy yellow chicks about one month after Hilda settled in. Palmer eagerly anticipated the moment the chicks would begin to hatch, as they'd be a welcome attraction at the children's activity farm he ran named — appropriately enough — Farmer Palmer's. He knew that there was nothing that children like more than watching a flock of baby chicks running around cheeping.

But when the eggs finally hatched, both farmer and hen got a big surprise.

They turned out to be Indian Runner ducklings, not chicks. Chickens and ducks congregate together at the farm and live in the same coops, so it seemed that Hilda had simply picked the wrong nest to sit on. Though Palmer had regularly checked the nest after he first saw the eggs, Hilda rarely left her perch, and so he had no idea they were duck eggs, which are significantly larger than chicken eggs.

As it turned out, it didn't much matter to the mother of her accidentally adopted children. Once the ducklings opened their eyes, they saw Hilda, and thanks to avian imprinting, they automatically regarded her to be their true mother, and the hen treated them as her own.

"Hilda doesn't seem bothered at all," said Palmer. "The ducklings follow her around just as chicks would. It was so surprising but lovely and she has proved to be very capable at raising them. The ducklings aren't aware that their mother is a hen, and Hilda is totally unaware that she's actually got a bunch of ducks waddling behind her."

Within a short time, five ducklings scurrying closely behind a hen became a regular sight at Farmer Palmer's. "The ducklings don't leave her side and if they get scared they run for cover under their 'mum,'" Palmer added.[1]

Family Fact: Ducklings are not born with waterproof down; an oil gland at the base of the tail develops later as they mature, helping to coat the feathers.

The Cat and Her Squirrel

The day started out like any other. Rebecca Hill was walking her three children to school in West Sussex in the United Kingdom, when they came across a squirrel, which was not unusual in their neck of the woods.

What was unusual, however, was the fact that the squirrel looked to be only a few days

old, and that it had clearly not eaten in awhile. In other words, the baby squirrel looked in danger of perishing right then and there.

Hill and her family were avid animal lovers who already had laid claim to two cats named Sugar and Spice, and so after dropping her children at school, Rebecca scooped up the squirrel and took him home, where she tried to feed it from a baby bottle. Unfortunately, the critter wanted nothing to do with it.

That's when Rebecca's husband, Martin, came up with an idea: Sugar and Spice had each given birth to a litter of five kittens — for a total of ten — a couple of weeks earlier, so maybe they could slip the squirrel in between the kittens and the nursing moms wouldn't notice. After all, the two cats were already sharing nursing duties with kittens roaming from one mama cat to the other, so what was one more mouth to feed, even if it belonged to a different species?

They decided to give it a chance. To facilitate the process, Martin came up with a novel solution: He decided to sprinkle some of Rebecca's perfume on the baby — specifically Chanel No. 5 — so that the cat wouldn't automatically view the squirrel as a threat to her and her babies, but rather a familiar part of the household. He figured that after a certain point, the cats' maternal instincts would kick in and both mothers would view the squirrel as just another one of the kittens.

It was worth a try, especially as the condition of the squirrel — now christened Chestnut by the children — was deteriorating further. Martin checked with the family's veterinarian, who said it couldn't hurt. "It was a bit of a gamble, but I sprayed him with perfume to disguise his smell," said Martin. "Chanel No. 5 is my wife's favorite and the cats seem to like it too."

After dousing the squirrel with perfume, they set Chestnut in among the kittens and watched and waited. "I was worried they might turn against him, but I watched them for a couple of hours and Chestnut was happily suckling," Martin reported. Within a few days, both Sugar and Spice were feeding and grooming Chestnut as if he was one of the litter.

The family began to add some fruit, nuts, and popcorn to the squirrel's diet as well, and Chestnut continued to thrive. "I'm sure Chestnut thinks he is a cat and the cats think so too," Martin added. "He plays rough and tumble with the other kittens and only leaves the basket to forage for other food. He still has that instinct. I found both cats after they'd been dumped in a plastic bag, so perhaps they look after Chestnut because they know what it's like to be abandoned."[1]

Family Fact: Squirrels are born without fur and teeth; but they have both by the time they're two months old. Depending on the type of squirrel, they become adults between ten and eighteen months of age.

The Boxer and His Kid

Elizabeth Tozer of the Pennywell Farm wildlife center at Buckfastleigh, in Devon, in the United Kingdom, was concerned in February 2008 when she checked in on the goat pen and saw that one of her female goats had just given birth to three kids. Goats have their hooves full dealing with two, and so in order to ensure that the two healthiest babies survive, the mothers will typically ignore the runt, which in most cases is left to die.

Tozer immediately got busy cleaning and bottle-feeding the baby kid. She was prepared to take over the role of mother herself, but then her male boxer dog named Billy surprised her by assuming parenting duties for the orphaned goat — who Tozer would christen Lilly — when she was just a few hours old. In fact, Tozer says that Billy's paternal instinct kicked in the instant he spotted Lilly. Right then he nosed Tozer away from Lilly and insisted on helping to clean and groom her. After he was done that first time, he never let the kid out of his sight, and vice versa.

Family Fact: When a mother goat — known as a doe — gives birth to twins of different sexes, the male is almost always born first.

"Lilly follows Billy around, which is really quite amusing to watch, and Billy sleeps with the goat and cleans her mouth after she feeds,"[1] said Tozer, adding that the unique relationship helped to attract a large number of curious visitors to the sanctuary.

The Springer Spaniel and Her Lambs

On a sprawling sheep farm, dogs have an important role to play. They can help out by herding other animals, they can scare away predators, and they serve as loyal companions who help out at the end of a hard day by just lying alongside their humans, and occasionally other critters, the satisfaction of a hard day's work behind them.

Few farmers would expect any canine to help out with feeding other animals on the farm, but that's exactly what a springer spaniel named Jess does on a 180-acre farm in Devon, Great Britain.

Jess feeds orphaned lambs on the farm by holding a bottle of milk in her mouth and letting the little ones go at it. Her owner, Louise Moorhouse, who keeps around 270 rare-breed sheep on the farm, including the Dorset Horn, said she doesn't know what she would do without the ten-year-old dog. "It's like having an extra pair of hands," she said.

At any one time, Jess serves as surrogate mother to several orphaned or abandoned lambs. "She's been doing it ever since she was a puppy," said Moorhouse, who admits she still laughs at the sight of Jess galloping across the field, milk bottle in mouth, in pursuit of a hungry lamb. "I taught her to hold the milk bottle in her mouth and she did the rest."[1]

Jess also makes herself useful with other skills, including toting buckets of water or grain, and even bringing tools to wherever Moorhouse sends her on the farm. In fact, Jess has become such a valuable — and beloved — dog to both humans and lambs that she is already helping to train a new recruit — a cocker spaniel named Lily — to ramble across the pastures and help to feed even more orphans and abandoned lambs who need her.

Family Fact: Springer spaniels shed year-round, so their owners should be prepared to groom them more regularly than other breeds.

The Kelpie and His Baby Chicks

When Maree Lousick's seven-year-old purebred kelpie named Murray went missing for hours each day from the home they shared in Darwin, Australia, she never grew worried. He always came back by the end of the day.

But one day, Murray didn't come home, and Maree went looking for him, driving all over the neighborhood. Her imagination ran wild, but she refused to give up. After spending hours calling his name, she headed home, hoping he had returned. Less than a mile from home, she finally spotted her dog, and just what he was doing would have never entered her mind in a million years.

Her beloved dog was sitting in a neighbor's yard playing with a flock of baby chicks.

Was that all? She called him into the car, and after a bit of coaxing, he climbed into the front seat and headed home with her. The next day, when he wandered off again, this time she knew where to look first. "When it happened again the next day, and the day after, it actually got a bit embarrassing," she admitted. "That's when I knew there was only one way to keep him at home: I had to buy him his own little chicks."

The next day, Lousick bought two little black chicks for her dog because they just happened to match his fur. And just like that, Murray's wandering days were over.

In fact, the dog became so attached to the chicks that he only left their side to go outside to relieve himself. Now, Lousick never wonders where her dog is as long as there are at least a couple of chicks in her home.

"While I'm at work, I keep the chicks in a little box in the house, and Murray sits next to the box all day and stares at it," she said. "When I come home we let them out and he plays with them on the lawn. They crawl all over him, slide off his head, he carries them around in his mouth and they never get out of his sight. He's a great dad to his chickens, he sleeps next to them, and at the slightest noise he's up to check up on them. He's even given up all his dog habits, like fetching things and playing with the ball, just to sit next to them.

"Murray is in love with his baby chickens."[1]

Family Fact: Hens like to lay their eggs in nests that have at least another egg or two; it's not unusual for two chickens to hatch each other's eggs in one nest at the same time.

The Golden Retriever
and Her Bunnies

One day in the spring of 2011, San Francisco resident Tina Case finally agreed to allow her daughters Danielle, Sami, and Alli to acquire a dog of their own if they a) promised to take care of it, and b) saved up the money necessary in order to bring one home. After receiving her permission, all three girls got busy, knocking on neighbors' doors to offer their pet- and babysitting services. Once they had saved up enough money, off they went to pick out a suitable canine.

They found Koa, a golden retriever who quickly settled into her new home. She set her mind to becoming an integral part of the family, offering companionship to the Cases who in turn provided her with plenty of opportunity to pursue more doggy pursuits. Soon Koa's favorite activity became chasing lizards in the

Family Fact: Female rabbits only spend about five minutes each day nursing their babies.

backyard, and to the little girls' relief, the dog always let the reptiles go after providing them with a little bit of exercise.

One day, Koa was on her usual lizard hunt when she became obsessed with exploring a raised spot of dirt alongside the house. Danielle and Sami came to investigate what their beloved dog was so intent on investigating, and to their great surprise, they found a nest full of wild baby rabbits. The girls rushed the bunnies to a neighbor who was also a vet, who diligently checked them over. After a thorough examination and clean bill of health, the bunnies were returned to the Case family along with instructions on how to care for them.

The girls and their mom were prepared to take care of the bunnies themselves, but then Koa stepped in to help care and nurture her discoveries. It was an unusual situation, because many breeds of dogs would rather chase rabbits than nuzzle them, but she was determined to protect them.

After some initial hesitation, Tina Case decided to allow the dog to exercise her maternal instincts. "Koa has never been a mother, so she thinks these are her little puppies," she said. "They hop all over her and always find their way to the crook of her leg and find warmth and shelter."[1]

The Cat and Her Ducklings

In 2007, a three-year-old Japanese cat named Hiroko gave birth to three kittens, but within a few days all three unfortunately died. Her owners, farmers Norio and Yoshiko Endo of Saitama Prefecture, took note but they had a busy farm to run and thought there was nothing they could do. By chance, they had recently purchased a pair of spot-billed duck eggs from another farmer, and when the ducklings hatched, they placed the birds in a separate room on the farm. The Endos were experienced farmers, and knew not to keep cats and ducks in the same vicinity, especially not in the same enclosure. But in the hectic daily life of running a farm, one day they accidentally shut the cat in the same room with the ducklings. When they went to check on the ducklings and saw the cat in the room, they immediately panicked.

But their alarm quickly turned to relief and surprise when they saw that Hiroko's maternal instincts were so strong that she had passed the care and nurturing she would have been providing to her own kittens directly onto the ducklings. After all, she had just lost her kittens and had no infant animals on which to focus her maternal urges until she saw the ducklings. So she instinctively began to groom and lick them and, since ducklings automatically imprint on the first creature they see after they open their eyes, they assumed that Hiroko was their mother.

To the relieved Endoes, it made perfect sense. And for both sides, it was literally love at first sight.

Family Fact: When you hear a duck quack, it's probably a female since most male ducks are mute.

The Hen and Her Falcon Chick

Falconer David Buncle, of Cheshire in the United Kingdom, was an expert in the ways of birds, as he had run an aviary of his own for more than twenty years. He was well-acquainted with their individual personalities and temperaments, so he could look at any one of his birds in his almost four-acre aviary and immediately see signs of contentment . . . or great trouble.

So when a four-year-old falcon named Shola prepared a nest, Buncle knew to keep a close eye and be prepared to spring into action. Shola — a rare breed known as a Laggar that is native to the Indian subcontinent — had abandoned her eggs numerous times in the past,

27

putting the species into even greater peril and even closer to extinction; it's estimated that only sixty of this breed exist in all of the United Kingdom, and fewer than ten thousand worldwide due to shrinking habitat and an increase in pesticide usage.

Shola laid her egg, but almost immediately started to spend a worrying amount of time away from the nest. This time, Buncle knew exactly what to do. He looked around his chicken house for a hen whose eggs would hatch around the same time as Shola's and simply moved the falcon egg to a nest belonging to a bantam hen named Tufty.

"It was the only way to keep him alive," said Buncle.

It worked. The egg hatched and the falcon chick was healthy. However, the time soon arrived for the newborn to start on the baby falcon equivalent of solid food.

Minced chicken.

"Tufty had the instinct to brood him, but not to feed him,"[1] said Buncle. Or at least not feed him in the best way for all involved.

So after Tufty had done her job, Buncle took over, moving the baby falcon, now named Pingu, into his own cottage until he turned about three months old. By this time, his wing-span had grown to approximately three feet, and he was ready to leave the nest.

Family Fact: Laggar falcons don't stray far from their homes.

The Border Collie and
His Vietnamese Pot-Bellied Piglets

The Blue Cross is known to be one of the largest animal welfare non-profits in the United Kingdom, and for many years dedicated staffers have become experienced at taking in abandoned animals of all types while also providing veterinary care and training assistance to the pets of local families.

Liz Grant was working at the Blue Cross animal hospital at Northiam near Hastings when, in April 1997, a client showed up with four newborn piglets. Sadly, their mother had rejected them. Grant

immediately sprang to action, wrapping them up, keeping them warm, and most importantly, feeding them. While she worked, a border collie named Mac — who served as the official greeter of all humans and animals at the veterinary hospital — came around to check out the new arrivals and welcome them.

"Mac soon made the quartet feel at home with plenty of licking and cuddling," said Grant, adding that the piglets accepted the attention and soon started climbing all over Mac and looked to her for guidance in the ways of everything from eating to play. "The piglets are lucky to be alive."[1]

Vietnamese pot-bellied pigs are known for their ability to get along well with people as well as with other animals. They are also smart and often take after dogs in their ability to learn tricks — from knowing how to walk and heel to enjoying a good game of fetch.

Who knows? After Mac's job was done and the piglets went off to their new homes, maybe one of them later returned the favor by helping to raise an abandoned puppy.

Family Fact: Purebred Vietnamese pot-bellied pigs are significantly smaller than the typical pig found on most farms. If one is significantly larger than a medium-sized dog, it has probably been interbred with a species of farm pig.

The Reed Warbler
and Her Cuckoo Chick

When wildlife photographer David Tipling witnessed a reed warbler feeding a cuckoo — a bird three times its size — in East Tilbury in Great Britain in June 2011, he knew he was watching an unique event in nature.

The cuckoo is what's known as a *brood parasite*. They lay their eggs in the nests of other birds and, in a chameleon-like fashion, their eggs change color to look like those that are already in the nest. By the time the chick hatches, the mother cuckoo has already flown the coop and is far, far away.

Most birds typically catch on to an intruder's egg, but if they don't, shortly after pecking his way through the shell, the newly hatched cuckoo would have taken matters into his own claws and by sheer virtue of his size, would overpower the others and elbow both parents and chicks out of the nest.

However, on that day in East Tilbury, none of this happened, to Tipling's great surprise. After the cuckoo hatched from the sole egg in the nest at the time — the warbler parents treated the cuckoo chick as if everything was business as usual, albeit in the form of a somewhat larger chick with different coloring. Still, they started to feed and care for the cuckoo.

"These reed warblers appeared to think the chick was their own, and it was just their instinct to look after it and feed it," said Tipling. "The cuckoo was three times the size of them but they didn't seem to notice. They even tried to keep it warm by sitting on it and covering it with their wings."

Despite the warbler parents' lack of prejudice — and fear — their nonchalance was bound to shift, and fast. Around eighteen days after hatching, the cuckoo chick typically develops the feathers and strength necessary to fly. At that point it would become so large as to flatten the nest, sending both warbler parents scrambling to find another home. But as Tipling put it, in the scheme of this rare case, it doesn't much matter.

"The warblers will just think they've raised a successful family,"[1] he said. Because the cuckoo easily ate three times the amount of bugs and worms of a standard warbler chick, the poor parents were tuckered out by the time the cuckoo flew the coop. Indeed, judging from the photographs, at times it looks as if the cuckoo could swallow his parents whole.

In that way, feeding the cuckoo isn't much different from human parents feeding a teenage boy.

Family Fact: A female cuckoo can lay up to twelve eggs in different nests over the course of a year.

The German Shepherd
and Her Kittens

When wildfires hit Victoria, the southwest area of Australia, in February 2009, rescue workers brought many injured and orphaned baby animals to veterinary hospitals in the region. One of the saviors they called upon was a woman by the name of Tracy Jamieson, who worked as a vet in the town of Frankston. When litters of kittens began to arrive in droves, Jamieson took them in and began to feed them with a bottle, but she quickly became over-

whelmed by the round-the-clock schedule of cleaning, attending to their injuries, and feeding them.

Fortunately, Luka, her four-year-old German shepherd, knew exactly what to do even though she had never had a litter of puppies of her own. The dog assumed responsibility for caring for the three five-week-old kittens—which Jamie-

son had named Emma, Ben, and Louise — like she had been doing it all her life, grooming and cleaning them, as well as allowing them to nuzzle up against her.

Indeed, Luka was so instantly comfortable with the tiny felines — and they with her — that when another litter of kittens arrived at the hospital the following week, Jamieson let Luka handle them as well.

The dog was now caring for six kittens, and all indications were that she was incredibly happy with her job. The second batch of kittens — named Hannah, Amelia, and Zak—were only two weeks old and instantly cuddled up to the German shepherd alongside their adopted littermates. Luka was immediately protective of every one of them.

"They are all gorgeous and in need of new homes," Jamieson said. "Although Luka will be sad to see them go."[1]

Family Fact: German shepherds have a double coat, where the outer coat consists of medium-length coarse fur that is shed on a regular basis, while the undercoat is softer, almost downy, and is rarely shed.

The Owl and Her Gosling

At the North East Falconry Centre in Aberdeenshire, Scotland, a fifteen-year-old owl named Gandolph was becoming increasingly upset and stressed in the spring of 2004. For years, each time she laid an egg in her nest and then dutifully sat on it for weeks on end, no chick had ever hatched.

John Barrie, who ran the center, had grown concerned about Gandolph's increased distress over the years. So when a neighbor gave him a goose egg, he decided to give it to Gandolph in the hopes it would help soothe her maternal angst, at least for a short while.

He knew the odds were against him and the owl. For one, it was highly unlikely that the egg was fertile. Next, it was doubtful that the owl's maternal instincts would kick in, since in the wild, birds will usually ignore an egg that is radically different from their own. Lastly, if Gandolph did proceed to nest and if it did miraculously hatch, most female owls would quickly realize that something was amiss once the first crack in the shell appeared, and typically kill the newborn, especially in the case of raptors such as owls.

But none of that happened. Instead, Gandolph became a surrogate mother to a gosling, who imprinted and considered the owl to be her natural mom. In turn, Gandolph cared for the baby goose, and her stress diminished considerably.

According to a spokesperson for the Royal Society for the Protection of Birds, this occurrence was a rare thing. "It's an incredible story," said the representative. "This kind of fostering does not happen in the natural world."[1]

Family Fact: There are two distinct classes of owls: barn owls, which have a characteristically heart-shaped face, and true owls, which have round faces.

The Goat and Her Wolf Pup

When some residents of Nanyu-anzi village, in Xinjiang, China, headed into the nearby woods to do some hunting, they ended up finding a newborn wolf pup nestling up against its dead mother. They took pity on the orphan and brought it back to the village. They knew one of their neighbors, Chen Ming, had a goat that had recently given birth, and they delivered the wolf pup to him in the hopes that there would be enough milk to nourish the wolf.

Not only was there sufficient milk, but the goat cared for the wolf like it was its own kid. Three years after neighbors first brought the wolf to Chen's house, the goat and wolf amazingly remained inseparable.

"They eat and sleep together," said Ming. "Everyone who comes to my home is surprised by the scene, that prey is very good friends with the predator."[1] He added that he wanted to release the wolf into the wild. However given the fact that the pair have been close since their initial introduction, he may not.

Family Fact: Wolf pups are born blind, but will open their eyes by the time they're two weeks old.

The Chicken, the Goose, and Their Three Ducklings

Doreen and David Bowman are farmers in Thayer, Iowa, and in their years of farming, they've seen Mother Nature take some unusual twists.

But nothing quite prepared them for what happened when two of their resident female birds — a chicken named Henrietta and a goose named Gertie — ended up raising a clutch of ducklings, making them quite the mixed family.

It all started when a mother duck on the farm was sitting on her own nest of eggs close to where Henrietta was nesting on her own eggs. Unfortunately, it didn't look like any of Henrietta's eggs were going to hatch, which had happened before. Once the first of the ducklings started to break through its shell in the adjacent nest, the mama

duck inexplicably stood up and left her nest. Henrietta watched the scene unfold, and after the mother duck had departed, the quick-witted hen quickly moved both duckling and the remaining unhatched duck eggs over to her own nest.

It's easy to imagine that Henrietta held her breath to see if the mama returned, but the duck never did. At the same time, though, another bird was also paying close attention to the proceedings: Gertie the goose, who had faced the same problems Henrietta had in hatching a brood of her own. A few hours later, when the ducklings were ready to leave the nest, they dutifully followed their adopted chicken mother out to explore. Gertie approached the group, essentially offering her assistance, and from that point on the family were bonded together.

"It was instant motherhood and they were a family from then on," said Doreen. "Whenever the ducklings make a sound like they're scared of something, both mothers instantly come running to the rescue."[1]

The two moms split parenting responsibilities: Henrietta handles care and feeding while Gertie naturally serves as swimming instructor and lifeguard, though Henrietta has actually been spotted in the pond trying to keep tabs on the ducklings.

Family Fact: Ducklings can swim as early as the day after they're hatched.

The German Shorthaired Pointer
and Her Owlet

Cherub, a white-faced scops owl, was four weeks old when he arrived at the Devon Bird of Prey Centre in Newton Abbot in Great Britain. Founder Karen Andriunas had acquired the owlet specifically for his size, since the scops is a miniature breed that won't grow much larger than a baby owl. Cherub's small size works perfectly for the educational demonstrations she regularly performs for area schoolchildren. "He is such a small owl so you can use him for school work because he is easy for the children to handle,"[1] she said.

Part of training owls and other birds involves letting them live at home and stretch their wings by flying around the house and some of the other buildings at the center, as well as getting them used to the various other birds and animals that call the center home. Andriunas has always been careful to keep a close watch on her dog Kiera, a German shorthaired pointer, whenever she introduces a new bird to the household.

Her caution is not surprising. While full-sized owl breeds are known to consider household pets as a good meal, the flip side is that pointers are generally known to be great all-purpose hunting dogs. And they don't make particularly good housemates with either cats or birds of any kind.

With Kiera, however, Andriunas needn't have worried. In fact, Kiera pretty much adopted the owlet from the first moment she set eyes on the baby. From then on, the dog rarely let Cherub out of her sight. When Andriunas began taking Cherub to schools with her, leaving Kiera back at home, the dog didn't relax until both Andriunas and the owl returned safely.

Family Fact: Female owls lay their eggs one at a time, over the course of several days, so the owlets are not born simultaneously.

The Tamarin Monkey
and His Twin Baby Marmosets

In most cases, monkeys can be notoriously breed independent. In other words, it's rare to see two different breeds of monkeys mix together, let alone step in to raise another monkey's babies.

"While it is well recorded that primates do often work together to assist the young of their own species, it is much more unusual to see this cooperation going on between different primate species,"[1] says Clive Barwick, the curator at the Colchester Zoo in Great Britain, where a golden lion tamarin monkey named Tom broke with tradition and took an active role in helping to raise a pair of silvery marmosets, a smaller breed of monkey. In March 2011, a pair of silvery marmosets named Olive and Arthur gave birth to twins, an unusual occurrence since most primates

tend to carry only one infant at a time. While monkey mothers take on the bulk of responsibility for feeding and caring for the baby, the father will often pitch in, as will members of the extended family. But rarely will a monkey of another species step in to shoulder some of the tasks.

Tom first took charge when the babies were around six weeks old; at that age, they would have grown too large for Olive to carry both at the same time. But given his larger size, carrying two at once was no burden for the male nanny, or "manny." In this way, Olive has simply followed the greater trend of female celebrities such as Madonna and Gwyneth Paltrow in depending upon a male caretaker to care for their young children.

Family Fact: Even though a group of marmosets can contain up to thirty different monkeys in the wild, there can be only one pair that breeds, since only the dominant female in the group will breed.

The Pointer Mix and His Joey

Rex is a ten-year-old German shorthaired and wirehaired pointer mix who happily kept his human, Leonie Allan, company in Torquay, a small seaside town in Victoria, Australia. "He's no angel, just an ordinary family dog with a bit of a naughty streak and a very gentle, passive, lovable temperament," said Allan.

One day, she and Rex went on their usual morning walk down the road where they both no-
ticed a dead kangaroo off to the side. The poor animal had been hit by a car, unfortunately not an uncommon occurrence in this part of the world. Allan figured local authorities would pick up the roo later that day, and when they returned home from their walk, she went outside to work in the garden and let Rex off his leash to wander around the yard.

Suddenly, Rex ran off toward the road. He returned minutes later carrying something in his mouth. "I was worried he'd found a snake and called him back, but then he dropped the joey at my feet," said Allan, who took a closer look, put two and two together, and realized the dead mother roo by the side of the road had left behind a baby that she estimated to be around four months old. "He obviously sensed the baby roo was still alive in the pouch and somehow had gently grabbed it by the neck, gently retrieved it and brought it to me," she said.

The two animals bonded quickly. Rex started licking and nuzzling the joey who responded by jumping and playing with the dog. They spent a few happy days together before the joey—christened Rex Jr.—was transferred to Jirrahlinga Koala Wildlife Sanctuary to be rehomed. Director Tehree Gordon marveled at Rex's nurturing approach toward the joey.

"That Rex was so careful and knew to bring the baby to his owners, and that the joey was so relaxed and didn't see Rex as a predator, is quite remarkable," she said. "It's a credit to the owners, who have taught him to be tolerant of the kangaroos, echidnas, and other animals that regularly come through their property. It's a lesson that dogs can be raised to be familiar and compatible with wildlife; you just have to teach them right from wrong."[1]

Family Fact: After it's born, a joey is not much larger than a lima bean; they generally stay in their mother's pouch for seven or eight months before first venturing out, though they may continue to nurse until they turn a year old.

The Great Dane and His Fawn

The men and women who work at Secret World Wildlife Rescue center, a sanctuary and rescue facility in Highbridge, Somerset, England, have seen many sick and injured animals brought in over the years, and they know the drill: Once the fox, owl, raccoon, or other animal makes it through the door, a team of experts quickly descends in order to diagnose and treat any problems before nursing it back to health with the eventual hope of releasing the animal back to the wild.

So when a days-old fawn came in who was deathly ill after apparently being being abandoned by her mother, the staffers sprang into action. "We found her in a terrible state," said Pauline Kidner, who founded the sanctuary with her husband Derek in 1984. "She was wet, cold and almost unconscious."[1]

Within a week, the baby deer had started to recover, and so Kidner began to bring the fawn—now named Cindy—outside for regular walks so she could regain her strength. Kidner's son had a Great Dane named Rocky who liked to check out the new arrivals, and once he took one look at the young fawn, the dog essentially muscled his way in to watch over Cindy.

The lovefest went both ways. "Rocky acts just like Cindy's mum," said Kidner. "And Cindy thinks Rocky is more likely than me to be her mother."[2]

Within two weeks of Cindy's arrival at the center, the two were inseparable, going on daily walks. Rocky acted as a mindful guardian and protector to the fawn, who would occasionally wander off to explore, but the moment she realized she was out of his reach, she

ran back to his side to nuzzle him and lean up against him.

"It's lovely to see," said Kidner.

Family Fact: Most fawns can stand up as soon as twenty minutes after they're born, and are able to walk within an hour of entering the world.

The German Shepherd Doberman Mix and His Baby Badger

Murray was a four-year-old German Shepherd Doberman mix who was happily living a life of greeting visitors and helping to supervise the intake of new animals at Secret World Wildlife Rescue animal sanctuary in Somerset, Great Britain, when a new arrival caught his eye in the spring of 1998. But it actually took another paternally minded canine for the two to meet.

Sometime in the previous week, a pet dog that was roaming the nearby countryside found a baby badger. The dog gently picked it up in its mouth and took it home to show his owners.

One look, and they knew things were rough for the young animal: It was underweight and greedily wolfed down the few scraps of food they had offered it before it started sniffing around for more. The couple had seen a dead badger by the side of the road earlier and figured that this one was newly orphaned. They called Pauline Kidner, the founder of nearby Secret World, who took the badger in and immediately started to care for the animal.

When the orphan arrived at the sanctuary, Murray took one look at the badger, and nosed Kidner out of the way. From that point on, the dog assumed the role of surrogate

father toward the badger cub—who Kidner named David—and the two were joined at the hip, or shoulder, from the very beginning.

"David certainly owes his life to one dog and loves playing with another," said Kidner. "Maybe he will come back in a second life as a dog."[1]

Family Fact: Badgers are nocturnal omnivores and can dig a hole in the dirt faster than a human.

The Border Collie and His Hyena and Tiger Cubs

As you have seen, with several of the surrogate animal parents in *One Big Happy Family*, the nurturing instinct is so strong in them that they will automatically reach out to parent any young critter that needs help, regardless of the species. In fact, the instinct is so innate that they'll do it time and again.

Solo, a tricolor border collie who lives at the Seaview Lion Park in Port Elizabeth, South Africa, is one of these animals. In fact, he'll spring into action and also care for baby animals of different species at the same time.

When a couple of orphaned hyena cubs first arrived at the park, Solo was already watching over a pair of four-month-old tiger cubs named Judo and Ruby, who had ended up at the park after they

were born prematurely. He helped clean them up and watched over them while they were being cared for by his human colleagues, before turning his attention to the hyenas.

Perhaps it's no surprise, since this energetic border collie, a breed known for its acute herding instincts, has no sheep or other livestock to herd at the lion park, and so he puts his energy into caring for the young animals in need.

"When orphans come into the farm, he definitely makes sure we are looking after them properly," says Ashley Gombert, general manager at the park, and Solo's owner. "He's even taken to grooming them."

He'll also try to herd them if they get too rambunctious. "Solo's border collie instincts will kick in sometimes, and he'll control them if they step out of line, but it shows that he is very caring," adds Gombert. "He's grown up around tigers, and he'll share his food with the tiger cubs, who will come and eat out of his bowl. But if they start eating too much, he'll snap at them and put them in their place."[1]

Family Fact: Baby hyenas — known as cubs — can nurse for up to one year.

The Lioness and the Antelope Calf

If you've seen even a handful of National Geographic or other wildlife documentaries, you know that eventually you're going to see a wild lion or tiger chase after a prey animal such as a zebra or antelope. Though you brace yourself for the inevitable — the attack and kill that you know is coming — the moment of attack still surprises, as does the horde of fellow animals in the pride or group who seem to immediately descend upon the fallen animal and make a good meal in no time at all.

So when wildlife photographer Adri de Visser watched two lionesses feeding on an antelope in Queen Elizabeth National Park in Uganda, he was not surprised as he watched the scene unfold through his lens. But what he saw next was like nothing he had ever witnessed.

After the lionesses finished their meal, they climbed up a tree to rest. De Visser heard a small noise like a cry. Moments later he saw a baby antelope emerge from the brush and realized it was the calf of the killed antelope.

The lions in the tree pricked up their ears — they had heard it as well — and one climbed down from her perch to investigate. When the calf saw the lioness, it ran up to her and poked its nose to her torso as if it was searching for milk.

"The lioness was really confused," said de Visser. The two animals started to check each other out—sniffing and licking; the lioness acted toward the baby antelope the way it would toward any of its cubs, albeit with a touch of hesitation. De Visser watched, utterly fascinated, taking pictures all the while to document the event.

About forty-five minutes later, the roar of a motorcycle popped through the silence, which startled both human and animals. A park ranger rode by, and the lioness picked the calf up by the nape of the neck like she would do with her cub and trotted off into the tall grass. De Visser knew she meant no harm; if she were intent on killing the baby, she would have aimed for the throat.

The story didn't end there: Says de Visser, "[Later that day] we heard from a group of tourists that the fawn was later spotted alive and well."[1]

Family Fact: An antelope's horns are hollow and permanent, unlike a deer, which sheds its antlers every few years.

The Foxhound and Her Fox Kits

With some animals, their drive to help baby critters — whether their own, or others of the same species, and even infants from other species — is so strong that you can't stand in their way, you just gotta let them at it. A foxhound named Mama is one of those dogs.

It all started in September 2011 at the LEO Zoological Conservation Center in Connecticut, when director Marcella Leone grew concerned when one of their animals, an African fennec fox named Fiona, became pregnant; she had given birth previously, but unfortunately she had a history of abandoning or eating her newborns. Leone realized the best solution was to find a female dog that had recently given birth and was close to weaning her own puppies to pitch in and nurse the fox babies. Since fennec foxes are small, the best surrogate canine for the job would be a small dog like a Chihuahua.

Several weeks before Fiona was due to give birth, Leone put out feelers through a local rescue group called Adopt-A-Dog, who soon located a dog named Mama with six puppies of her own at a shelter in North Carolina. In fact, Mama's mothering instinct was so strong that it's the reason why she ended up in the shelter in the first place: The dog had tried to gather up six more stray puppies she found wandering around the streets and caused a car accident.

Everything sounded fine until Leone saw a picture of the dog: Not only was Mama larger than a Chihuahua, the dog was an American foxhound, which is bred to, *ahem*, hunt foxes. Leone had her doubts, but once she heard about Mama's maternal streak, she thought perhaps that it would override her breed instincts, so she decided to give it a try.

Volunteers relayed Mama and her puppies from North Carolina to Connecticut, where they prepared the puppies for adoption while Mama headed to the LEO headquarters; they made it through the door just as the fox kits were born, and staff and foxhound prepared for action.

When Mama first saw the fox kits, she growled and had to be held back, but staffers were patient. They placed the kits in an incubator and brought them out to nurse every two hours. In the beginning, one person would hold Mama's head and distract her while another held her down by her hips. A third person then brought the kits up to Mama's teats because they were too small to reach them on their own. Though it took an hour the first time, soon everyone — humans, kits, and dog — got used to the process and relaxed.

And just as Leone expected, Mama's maternal instincts overrode her hunting drive.

"She loved them and cleaned them and protected them," Leone said. "She is just a precious, wonderful dog."[1]

Family Fact: Most foxes breed from December through February, and the only time an adult fox will sleep in a den is when a female — called a vixen — is nursing her young.

The Cow and Her Lambs

On a small farm in Pencarrow, New Zealand, back in 2001, it wasn't an unusual sight to see two tiny lambs following a two-and-a-half-year-old Jersey cow named Little Brown around the pasture.

That's because after the two lambs were rejected by their mother, Mike and Tina Pizzini knew they had to take quick action. They introduced the two newborn lambs — who were born on Christmas Day 2000 — to Little Brown when it was clear that their mother would not be able to fulfill her maternal duties.

For her part, Little Brown stepped right in and accepted the babies right from the beginning. All day long, the lambs were never too far from her side, and the surrogate mother cow would happily oblige the lambs whenever they wanted to eat or just nuzzle.

Three months after their introduction, the three were still as close as ever.

Family Fact: While humans have a vision radius of about 170 degrees, sheep can see up to 270 degrees around them.

Family Fact: When a monkey smiles, yawns, or nods quickly, it's considered a sign of aggression.

The Dog and His Baby Monkey

Human fathers — and mothers — across history have not hesitated to step in when one of their offspring is bullied or taunted by other children in the schoolyard or neighborhood. In 2008, a dog assumed the same role for a baby monkey at a zoo in Jiaozuo, in the Chinese province of Henan, when the youngster was constantly being bullied by adult monkeys in his enclosure.

The story began after the baby had lost both its parents. The other monkeys — both large and small — perhaps felt threatened by the orphan, and so they started to bully and attack the poor youngster. In fact, he was almost killed a couple of times.

Zookeepers decided to take action and placed a dog named Sai Hu into the monkey enclosure, figuring that the dog could help to protect the monkey and even distract the other monkeys before they could focus on the baby.

It worked. The baby monkey latched on to the dog by climbing onto his back minutes after Sai Hu entered the monkey area. Sai Hu also immediately assumed the role of surrogate father by standing up to the other monkeys when they began to taunt his newfound child.

In time, they became inseparable, and both the other monkeys and human visitors to the zoo took notice of the remarkable pair.

Family Fact: Dalmatians are bred to get along well with horses, since originally their primary job as firehouse dog was to run alongside the horse-drawn fire trucks to clear a path on the way to a burning building, and to help keep the horses calm while the firefighters did their job.

The Dalmatian and Her Lamb

John and Julie Bolton breed Dalmatians on a farm in Barossa Valley, Australia. They've seen a lot of interesting things in their years of raising dogs and sheep on the farm, but when they saw a ewe push away one of its newborn lambs and refuse to let it nurse with the others, a miraculous thing happened: Their Dalmatian Zoe stepped in to help.

In fact, once the two were introduced, Zoe—who was in heat at the time, but didn't get pregnant—assumed sole responsibility for caring for the lamb.

"Zoe is actually cleaning it and licking it and mothering it, and it tries to mother up to her udder," said Julie. "The lamb follows the dog but it gets its milk from me from the bottle."

The lamb is a cross between the sheep breeds of Dorper and Van Rooy, and the genetic pattern is identical to that of a Dalmatian. "It is truly spotted," said Julie. "Black spots on a white-based coat, which is the same as a Dalmatian."

"We're not quite sure what we should call it, whether it's a 'sheep-matian' or a 'Dal-dorper!'" joked her husband, John.[1]

For his part, the tiny lamb doesn't much care. Whether he thinks he's a dog or a lamb—or a combination of the two—once he latched onto Zoe and never strayed far from her side, things quickly progressed to the point where the lamb started sleeping inside the dog kennel happily nuzzled up against his "mother."

Family Fact: A chicken's resting heart beats from 250 to 300 times a minute; by contrast, the resting heart rate of a healthy adult human can range from 60 to 100 beats per minute.

The Cat and Her Baby Chicks

Though there's no proof that a surrogate mother or father is more likely to accept a young animal of another species under their wing if they bear some kind of resemblance — as in the case of Zoe the Dalmatian and the identically spotted and patterned lamb — it's easy to think that the similarity wouldn't hurt. That indeed was the case with Nimra, a one-year-old mother cat who was tending her litter of four kittens in Madaba, Jordan, when she adopted a flock of seven baby chicks that were suddenly orphaned in 2007 after their mother died.

Many of the chicks were the same color as Nimra, a ruddy dark orange, and so the possibility that she may have taken them under her wing, so to speak, could have been increased simply because they matched the pattern of her own coat.

Whatever the explanation, the cat that adopted chicks, accepting them alongside her new kittens, shocked onlookers in this city just south of Amman. Though she only nursed her own kittens, she treated the young chicks the same way as her own brood: Whenever a chick happened to stray, Nimra stopped whatever she was doing to head the young bird off at the pass. She then gently took the chick into her mouth and deposited it back in the cardboard box where she attended to her large brood, both chicken and feline.

The Mutt and Her Bush Baby

Judy was one of several resident dogs at a small zoo near Tamworth, Staffordshire, England. As she had been orphaned herself, the zookeepers thought she was ideally suited to serve as the surrogate mother for a fellow orphan — a bush baby — who was recently born at the zoo but had unfortunately been abandoned by its mother, not an uncommon event for primates born in captivity.

Infant bush babies have several special needs that set them apart from the newborn offspring of other species.

First: They are nocturnal, so they sleep during the day and will go out and about at night.

Second: For most of their waking hours, they have to cling to whatever creature is serving as their parent, for both physical and emotional needs and proper development.

This presented a bit of a dilemma for zoo staffers: They tried to teach the baby to cling to a wide variety of different objects, ranging from fluffy toys to a fur-covered hot-water bottle, but the infant would not be soothed no matter what they tried.

That's when they thought of Judy. However, in order to make their plan work, they had to make sure that the dog was comfortable with being in a dark room with a small furry creature that's particularly active. They also had to convert the bush baby's schedule so that it would coincide with the regular working hours of the staff.

First, though, they had to make sure that Judy wouldn't mind having a small sharp-clawed creature clinging tightly to her head. Happily, the dog passed the first test, and from the moment the bush baby was set onto her head like a big furry hat, Judy didn't seem to mind the warmth or the constant company. If she was at all uncomfortable, Judy never gave up her position by trying to dislodge the bush baby from his perch. And for his part, the bush baby seemed comfortable with Judy as well as the warmth and comfort she supplied.

Next, the zookeepers altered the lighting in the bush baby's room so that its nighttime occurred during the human's day, but they also had to shift Judy's schedule so that she in essence turned into a night owl. Zookeepers rigged the lighting system in the bush baby's enclosure so that the baby's nighttime ran roughly concurrent with actual daylight hours. That switch meant that they could keep tabs on his health, as well as check for any possible puncture wounds on Judy's head.

Once it was clear that the bush baby was starting to grow and thrive, staffers set about weaning him. After his mother had rejected him, the zoo stepped in to feed him with substitute bush baby milk from a tiny bottle. When it came time to wean him, he started in on the traditional bush baby diet of insects.

After eating, the bush baby exercised by jumping across the room in eight-foot-long bounds. But old habits die hard, and he would quickly return to cling to Judy.

Family Fact: The bush baby has two tongues, one for eating and a smaller grooming tongue of cartilage underneath to help keep its fur clean.

The Airedale Terrier
and Her Guinea Pigs

In Vancouver, British Columbia, an Airedale terrier named Sunshade is perhaps the most patient dog in the world.

Elaine Hu had gotten the dog for her sixteenth birthday in 2000, and they've been together ever since, essentially joined at the hip. Hu even started a blog — www.sunshadethesuperdale.com — featuring her best friend. On their regular trips to the

pet store for food and toys, Hu noticed that whenever they got close to the guinea pig cages, Sunshade would park herself right in front and just stare.

While some might think it was because of the breed — after all, Airedales are bred to chase and kill vermin of all types — Hu knew differently just by looking at Sun-

shade's body language. Whenever the dog spotted a squirrel or mouse in the yard, her entire body would tense, her ears would be alert, and she'd close her mouth tightly—all clear signs of a dog in the moments before an attack.

However, whenever Sunshade looked at a guinea pig, her body language was the exact opposite: She was totally relaxed as she watched the small critters, intrigued and curious, almost like she wanted to make friends.

In 2010, Sunshade was diagnosed with cancer, and thankfully was successfully treated. Afterward, Hu decided to give her beloved dog a present: a guinea pig of her own. After all, she thought her dog had waited long enough. So she brought home one guinea pig as a test, and Sunshade was so happy and nurturing toward the guinea pig that a month later, Hu bought her dog a second one.

Sunshade was in heaven, and helped out with their care and grooming. She clearly became sad whenever a pig left her side. As it turned out, one of the pigs happened to be male, and before long, a litter of baby pigs were born. Sunshade took care of this second generation—her step-grandchildren—as well. Hu decided to honor the incredible relationship her Airedale had with the guinea pigs by chronicling them on her blog and Web site.

Sunshade carried on happily until one of the babies unexpectedly died during the winter of 2012. Then an amazing thing happened: When Hu buried it in the backyard, Sunshade followed her, and then wouldn't leave the graveside. She mourned for several weeks, but rallied; after all, she still had other babies to look after.

Family Fact: The Airedale is known as the King of the Terriers, since it is the largest of the breed.

The Sow and Her Kitten

In farms all over the world, barn cats earn their name in a most appropriate fashion: They live in the barn and their primary job is to keep out the vermin.

Occasionally you'll find a farmer who takes pity on the outdoor felines, especially in cold climates, and will allow the barn cats to shift into the comparatively luxurious life of a house cat, at least during the coldest months.

And sometimes, you'll hear about a cat who refuses such creature comforts and instead prefers to lead a life in the outdoors, regardless of the weather.

That's precisely the case with a female tabby cat that roamed the farm and barns belonging to William Headley, a farmer in Norfolk near King's Lynn, Great Britain. The mother feline gave birth to a litter of kittens in the barn alongside several sows, one of which had just given birth to a clutch of newly born piglets of her own. Headley and his family grew concerned for the welfare of the cat family, and so moved them inside the farmhouse, at least until the kittens were able to survive on their own.

But the mother cat would have none of it. She immediately moved her kittens back to the barn. She clearly preferred the company of pigs instead of the humans.

The sows welcomed their old roommates back, as they were already used to having the cat and kittens nearby. In fact, the nursing sow did more than just greet them: When one of the kittens pushed her way in alongside the piglets to nurse, the mother pig allowed the baby cat to join right in. The piglets even played with the kitten, though none of the other cats joined her.

In time, the kittens grew to the point where they were able to head off to new homes. However, to avoid a repeat of the time when her mother had refused his hospitality, Farmer Headley thought it would be best if he kept the kitten who thought she was a pig. And so the kitten stayed behind, hanging out with her feline mother, but spending a good majority of her time with her adoptive mother and the piglets, even after the would-be siblings grew to outweigh and tower over her.

Family Fact: In the United Kingdom, a group of kittens is known as a kindle, while a collection of adult cats is a clowder.

The Pointer Rhodesian Ridgeback Mix and Her Baby Llama

Reg Bloom raised Peruvian llamas at his farm near Brightlingsea, Essex, in Great Britain. One day, a llama who had just given birth for the first time refused to feed its newborn, who had been named Mahogany. The farmer wasn't surprised, since the mother llama had been rescued and llamas normally learn how to nurse their young by watching others in the herd, an experience she obviously had missed.

Normally, a newborn in this situation would be bottle-fed by humans around the clock, but at the time Bloom's farm had so many other animals to care for that there weren't enough people to help handle the task.

That's when Bloom turned to his dog Rosie, a mix between a pointer and a Rhodesian ridgeback, who had just finished weaning her litter of pups. It was an unusual idea, but the hopeful farmer decided to at least give it a shot. Happily, Rosie took to the task like the proverbial duck to water. Bloom chalked it up to her previous experience nursing and helping to raise several orphaned and abandoned lion and tiger cubs that had come into the farm. She had a special knack for motherhood.

Though Rosie had previously done her duty and watched the cubs successfully move on after she'd weaned them, her relationship with Mahogany turned out to be quite different. Both dog and llama appeared to genuinely enjoy each other's company, and even though the time came when the llama grew bigger than this already substantial dog, they still shared a close, nurturing relationship even months after Rosie ceased to nurse her.

In fact, the entire Bloom family welcomed the relationship between the two: Mahogany would accompany Rosie on her nightly walks with the Blooms, who in turn allowed both dog and llama to sleep together at night in a spare room off the kitchen.

Family Fact: A baby llama, known as a **cria***, generally gains about a pound a day for the first three months of its life.*

The Boxer and Her Piglet

At the Hillside Animal Sanctuary in Norfolk, Great Britain, founder Wendy Valentine has seen more than her fair share of abused, abandoned, and orphaned animals come through her doors over the years. And while she and her staff do everything they can to help bring the unfortunate animals back to health, sometimes some extra assistance shows up where they least expect it.

One day, just a few days before Christmas 2011, a local rescuer found an hours-old piglet lying on the side of a road near the sanctuary. Valentine speculated that the feisty pig either got loose from a nearby pig farm or perhaps a sow had given birth while on a truck on the way to the slaughterhouse and the piglet fell through the slats on the trailer and onto the road.

"She was so small her umbilical cord was still attached," said Valentine. "We had to feed her by hand, and I brought her into the house with me so I could keep an eye on her."

Valentine's five-year-old boxer dog Susie—who she had rescued from a Welsh puppy farm a few years earlier—came by to check out the new arrival, and it was love at first sight. "It was obvious Tabitha [the name that the baby piglet was given] saw Susie as a mother

figure," she said. "Tabitha wouldn't stay away from the basket she was in, so I let them play together and they'd nuzzle up together and wouldn't leave each other's side."[1]

Though the pig soon grew to become the same size as Susie, their play together didn't change. "They just took an instant shine to each other and now are always together, even curling up to sleep with each other and eating next to each other," said Valentine. "It is really a wonderful relationship to witness. It seems they are absolutely besotted with each other. Susie is very gentle with her—it's almost like she instinctively knows she's just a baby. Sometimes they race around, rolling on their backs playing, and you can't help but smile."[2]

Family Fact: Pigs lack the physical ability to sweat, so they love to wallow in mud to cool off.

The Chimpanzee and Her Puppies

Animal lover Raymond Graham Jones ran a small wildlife park near Daventry, England. There was always a number of cats, dogs, and birds underfoot, some of whom took a keen interest in checking out any and all new arrivals that made it through the door.

He fully encouraged his more domesticated household pets to become acquainted with the wilder residents that he kept in the zoo. In time, he became a regular Doctor Dolittle, living in harmony with both wild and tame animals in his house. And Jones's mood always brightened whenever a friendly relationship between a wild animal and one of his domestic animal companions took root.

He often had several chimpanzees on the premises, but was always careful to keep a watchful eye over them whenever they interacted with another animal, because he had often found them to be generally unreliable when they handled small animals. In several cases, when a chimp became bored or distracted, he'd sometimes display hostile or threatening behavior toward the young animal or even drop it.

However, one chimp that Jones never had to worry about was named Anna, a primate who not only had a much better attitude toward other animals at the zoo, both large and

small, but clearly possessed extremely strong maternal instincts. She never ceased to be fascinated whenever a new puppy was born to one of the resident dogs. As Jones usually had several dogs breeding at a time, it essentially became a full-time occupation for Anna to help the mothers with their puppies.

Anna liked to watch the puppies while they nursed. After a pup had been fed by its mother, Anna would gently pick it up and cuddle it as if it was one of her own. And whenever a stranger would get too close to the pups, Anna would pop over and act very protective of the litter.

Most of the canine mothers grew familiar with Anna, and they realized the chimp was not a threat, since she always treated all the pups with great care and affection. Plus, perhaps the mama dogs realized that she gave them a bit of a break.

Family Fact:
Chimpanzees have more in common with humans than with gorillas, since we share between 95 and 98 percent of our DNA.

The Fox and Her Kittens

As a farmer in Norfolk, England, Ron Bayliss was accustomed to protecting his animals—including chickens, dogs, and cats—from the fox packs that regularly roamed around the perimeter of his land. But when he found a six-week-old fox kit in poor condition on his land, he decided to shift gears.

It was likely that the young female fox had wandered away from her mother and couldn't find her way back. When Bayliss rescued it in a field near his home, the fox was exhausted and close to death.

He took the cub home, fed it with a mixture of raw eggs and milk, and made a rudimentary bed and incubator on a shelf above his kitchen stove. After several weeks of care and nutrition, the fox gained some weight and started to become curious about the world around her, including the other animals on the farm. Though Bayliss had considered releasing the fox back to the wild after she recovered, he began to have second thoughts as April—named after the month when he had found her—was acting more like a domesticated animal than a wild critter.

April happily established herself in the farmhouse alongside Bayliss's several cats and small dogs and chowed down on dog food, cookies, and leftovers the animals shared from the same bowl. April also got herself into the rhythm of farm life, following Bayliss and his family as they went about their daily rounds on the farm, and she accompanied them on walks to exercise their dogs, wearing a collar and lead just like the canines. The farmer initially kept the fox away from the ducks and chickens on the farm, but after a short while, he discovered he needn't have worried; despite the old saying about the fox in the henhouse, April pretty much ignored the birds on the farm.

In fact, Ron's wife, Jenny, thought their adopted fox acted more feline than anything else. "April has never harmed anything in her life, not even mice," she said. "Perhaps she thinks she's a cat." Indeed, since April grew up with a number of cats and kittens, in time, it became common for her to assume special care for a kitten whenever one of the mother cats had a litter on the farm. And since the moms were already used to April, they were perfectly comfortable with having this special fox watch over the kittens.

"Cats and foxes seem strange bedfellows," Jenny added, "but when they romp together in the garden it's usually the cats who are chasing the fox."[1]

Family Fact: Although the fox belongs to the Canidae family — as do dogs — their behavior can be catlike, from the way their eyes narrow to the way they arch their backs and move sideways in a threatening situation.

The German Shepherd
and Her Bengal Tiger Cubs

When torrential rains hit Windsor, Australia, a town not too far from Sydney, in the spring of 2001, it was every man, woman — and animal — for themselves.

Unfortunately, in the case of wild animals who were raising newborns, some of those young critters had to fend for themselves. Some didn't survive, but four Bengal tiger cubs did more than just survive. They found a new home with Dr. Rob Zammit and his wife, Fiona Fearon, both animal experts and TV presenters in Australia. It was particularly important to save the cubs because at the time, the population of Bengal tigers worldwide was said to be less than 1,000 — today, National Geographic Society estimates that figure at around 2,500 — so every life saved presented a huge difference.

But the help extended to the tiger cubs didn't stop with the humans of the household: The Zammits' German shepherd, Pepper, also eagerly stepped into the fray.

"We made the decision to look after them ourselves and foster them, and Pepper decided that she'd help too, because there are a lot of things to be done,"[1] said Dr. Zammit.

The Zammits took care of feeding responsibilities since Pepper couldn't nurse their charges. But she did help out in a number of other ways.

"Pepper has been watching over them while they've been here and they all play happily together," Dr. Zammit said. "She has taken up many of the normal housekeeping duties of the cubs' parents, which include cleaning the cubs and supervising their toilet training."[2]

According to Zammit, Pepper and the tiger cubs like to spend their evenings relaxing in front of a good movie. Their favorites? *The Tigger Movie* and *The Lion King*.

Family Fact: Tiger cubs stay with their mothers for up to three years.

The Bulldog
and Her Baby Squirrels

One day in Warwickshire, England, a man named Leslie Clews went out to check to see how his garden had fared after a particularly nasty storm had passed through the night before. His flowers and vegetables made it through the wind and rain, but the garden's fauna had not been so lucky. On a patch of grass he found three baby squirrels that had apparently been abandoned by their mother after they fell out of a tree during the storm.

He took them inside and started to gather the materials and equipment necessary to feed them with milk squeezed through a pipette. But when he told a fellow animal lover about his intentions, he was advised against his plan as he thought they were unlikely to survive without their mother.

Clews didn't want to give up hope for the baby squirrels, and so he had an idea. Susie the family bulldog had recently given birth to three pups, and the day was coming for them to go off to their new homes. Though he was fully aware of how much dogs loved to chase squirrels, he decided to take a chance.

He set them down next to Susie in her basket, and stood back and watched. Within minutes, the squirrels were nursing, and Susie accepted them wholeheartedly, like the ba-

bies were just another litter she'd had. The squirrels picked up where the pups left off, and indeed, it almost seemed as though they had never left.

When photographer John Drysdale arrived to photograph the unusual adoption, he set up his cameras and was ready to shoot a picture of just the squirrels by themselves in the basket when all of a sudden Susie noticed what was going on. She rushed in to protect her new "pups," and only after a good deal of time had passed did she allow Drysdale to get his shots.

Family Fact: It's estimated that more than 80 percent of bulldog mothers give birth via Caesarean section because bulldogs today are bred to have such big heads.

The Orangutan and His Lion Cubs

Dogs are commonly used in zoos and wildlife sanctuaries around the world to help bring up abandoned lion and tiger cubs. But at Myrtle Beach Safari in South Carolina, a three-year-old male orangutan named Hanama has shaken things up a bit when it comes to expectations of which kinds of animals can help soothe baby animals who are in most need of food and comfort.

Whenever an animal is about to give birth at the park, a team of zoological specialists keeps close watch on the mother and the newborns; when the babies emerge into the world and take their first breaths, the staffers remove them from their mothers, which they believe increases their chances of surviving in captivity. So when a pair

of male cubs named Skukuza and Simh first met Hanama on the grounds of the wildlife park, the orangutan moved right in and scooped them up into his arms.

"Hanama is very smart and he was brought in to help babysit the cubs," said park director Dr. Bhagavan Antle. "He took to them straight away and watches over them as they play. He runs about with them and hangs out with them and sometimes picks them up to give them a cuddle. He'll balance them in his arms and shows them a lot of love."

When it comes to these — and other — young cubs, Hanama's fatherhood responsibilities continue for several months until the cubs grow too large for him to handle. "It's inevitable that they'll grow apart," Antle added. "In about six or eight months they'll get too big and Hanama won't be able to care for them any more."[1]

At that point, the paternal-minded orangutan will keep an eye out for the next opportunity to serve as the primary caretaker for newborns who need a father figure.

Family Fact: Orangutans primarily live in trees, and their diet consists mostly of fruit, including mangoes and figs.

Family Fact: Though the average length of a bush baby is only six inches, they can jump as far as twenty feet due in part to their powerful hind legs.

The Baboon and Her Bush Baby

The people who work at the Nairobi Animal Orphanage in Kenya have seen a steady stream of orphaned animals come in over the years, whether the mothers abandoned their young ones or had the misfortune to be killed, which is a common occurrence in the jungles of Africa.

So when a three-month-old bush baby—a small nocturnal primate also known as a galago—came into the orphanage, the staffers immediately got to work, checking its health, feeding it, and finding a place for it to stay on the grounds.

What they didn't expect is for one of the other residents at the orphanage, a seven-month-old yellow baboon, to swoop in and start to treat the orphan—who zookeepers had named Gakii—as if he was one of her own babies.

"This is not normal," said Edward Kariuki, who works at the orphanage. "It has not happened here and I guess it has not happened anywhere else."

But that doesn't much matter to the baboon and Gakii. They rarely leave each others' sides, they drink milk together from the same bowl, and Gakii crawls all over the baboon—that is, when the surrogate mother is not tightly holding the tiny bush baby in her arms.

The Yellow Lab and His Duckling

Mountfitchet Castle, in Stansted, Essex, England is a very special place for humans and animals alike. The castle is a National Historic Monument that has taken on a new life to serve not only as a reconstructed medieval castle and Norman village, but also as a sanctuary for abandoned and rescued animals who roam around the ten-acre grounds.

Director Jeremy Goldsmith considers himself to be caretaker to both castle and critters, and he's pretty much prepared to deal with whatever happens to come down the pike. One day in the spring of 2012, a duckling showed up after its mother had been killed by a fox. From the time the downy orphan showed up, Goldsmith's yellow Lab, Fred, quickly got to work helping the duckling — soon named Dennis — to recover from his trauma.

"When we found Dennis, he was quite frail and he clearly would not have survived another day on his own," said Goldsmith. "Fred, who has always been extremely loving, went straight up to him and began to lick the little bird clean. Since then Dennis has not stopped following him around and Fred has pretty much adopted him."

The duckling likes to cozy up to the dog in the evening. They play together, and on occasion, Fred will accompany Dennis as he glides through a pond near the castle, though

Goldsmith admits that the duck is a little more nimble paddling around than his four-legged surrogate father.

"I don't think the duckling would have made it without Fred," said Goldsmith. "His loving nature really does make a difference."

Not every dog would have been so welcoming of a feathered creature. After all, some Labs are prized as extremely skilled duck hunters. Fred was different. Ever since he was a puppy, he became accustomed to being surrounded by many different types of animals. He also nosed his way into helping to raise whatever creature most needs it at the castle. Goldsmith says that he pitched in to care for a deer awhile back.

"Dennis absolutely adores Fred so I am sure he will pick up some canine traits, so I fully expect him to start barking and chasing cats shortly," said Goldsmith, who adds that he thinks Dennis views Fred as more mother than father. "In that way, I suppose he is a bit like one of those modern stay-at-home dads."[1]

Family Fact: Ducks have no problem swimming in cold water since their feet have neither blood vessels nor nerves.

The Chicken and Her Rottweiler Puppies

At a farm in Shrewsbury, England, a hen named Mabel paid her owners, Edward and Ros Tate, back for saving her from being dinner by helping to raise some of the other animals around the farm. Specifically, she focused on a litter of four newborn Rottweiler puppies whose mom, Nettie, particularly needed the extra help.

It all started when a chick was born in the henhouse. Edward said her fate was to eventually end up on someone's plate, but a fateful encounter with a horse on the farm was the thing that saved her life. The horse stepped on her foot, causing nerve damage that made her especially sensitive to the cold in winter, so the Tates named her Mabel — most farmers only give names to animals they intend to keep as pets, not those they send to market — and brought her inside.

Their dog, Nettle, had recently had a litter of puppies, and while she took care of the rudimentary tasks like nursing and a little grooming, it seems she was far more interested in getting back to her premotherhood schedule: wandering around the farm and seeing what's new.

Whenever Nettle nestled with her puppies, Mabel watched intently. But when the mother dog went outside for a break, Mabel saw her chance, and she pounced into the basket of puppies to keep them warm, although truth be said, they probably helped keep the hen warm as well. The family was quite shocked when it first happened — to say nothing of Nettle the first time she came back into the house and saw a chicken sitting on her puppies. But everyone quickly adjusted: puppies, mom, and chicken.

"She took to them like they were her own chicks," said Edward. "Nettle was a bit startled to say the least, but she didn't mind too much eventually. She's happy to have a helping pair of wings. We're hoping that soon Mabel will have her own chicks to look after but I don't think Nettle will be returning the favor when that happens."[1]

Family Fact: The Rottweiler is one of the oldest dog breeds, dating back to ancient Rome, though they first became popular in Germany where they were bred to help herd and drive cattle.

The Chihuahua and
His Baby Marmoset

A Chihuahua named Sam inadvertently became a surrogate mother of sorts to a young marmoset at a small zoo near Thetford, Norfolk, England. The zoo was part of an estate at Kilverstone Hall where overseers Lord and Lady Fisher ran a breeding program designed to save certain Latin American animals largely considered to be endangered. As is often the case with animals born in captivity, a few members of the marmoset group started fighting with each other, and rather than risk having something unfortunate happen to the youngest marmoset, Sam was called into service on a daily basis to take the small primate for a ride outdoors where he could get some much-needed sunlight and exercise, as well as satisfy its innate physical and emotional need to cling to a larger, warm, furry creature.

It wasn't the easiest job in the world for the Chihuahua. Sam only weighed a few pounds himself, and so the baby marmoset — who may have tipped the scales at three ounces — still proved to be a burden to the small dog, not to mention the fact that the marmoset held onto the Chihuahua pretty tightly. Its sharp claws couldn't have been comfortable to Sam.

Fortunately Sam had a backup marmoset carrier on call in the form of a golden retriever

who was also used to ferry the lucky, well-cared-for marmoset around.

Family Fact: Chihuahuas were originally bred to be companion dogs, and their portable size fits their personality, since they love nothing better than to be with their humans 24/7.

The Peacock and Her Gosling

The mother peacock may have thought she was sitting on her own eggs, but in the end she ended up nesting on a pair of goose eggs owner Caroline Halse had received from some friends to serve up for the morning meal at her bed and breakfast.

"We didn't know if the eggs were fertilized because they had been bought from a shop, so as a joke I decided to see if Valentine [the mother peacock] would sit on them," said Halse, adding that she'd always wanted to add a goose to her menagerie at How Park Farm, her small inn near Stockbridge, Great Britain. "They were so large that I wasn't sure if she would sit on them, but she did for thirty-one days and then this tiny yellow thing came out."

As it turned out, one of the eggs was unfertilized, but the other one hatched. If Valentine suspected something was out of sorts, she didn't let on, as she nested and nurtured the rather large chick for several days before introducing Goosey—as Halse christened her—to the joys of grubbing for bugs and worms in the garden.

"Valentine is a fantastic mum, very protective," said Halse. "She walks it around, shows it what to eat, and even puts it to bed at night. She even tried to attack me when I once tried to pick the gosling up.

"She hasn't had any chicks of her own for two years, so it was rather nice for her to have Goosey Gander this year. I do think Valentine will teach Goosey to fly, but it's going to be interesting to see if Goosey will learn how to be a goose or a peahen."[1]

Family Fact: Geese make great watchdogs, since they tend to honk at anyone or anything they consider to be intruding on their space. They attack by hissing loudly, lowering their head so it's parallel to the ground, and running toward the offender.

The Labrador and Her Baby Pygmy Hippo, Her Tiger Cubs, Her Porcupine, and . . .

Like Jasmine the greyhound in Great Britain, who helped raise a variety of different species of animal babies, Lisha is another canine mom who had gotten off to a rough start when she was young.

Lisha is a Labrador retriever who lives with owners Nadine and Rob Hall in the Oudtshoorn region of South Africa. By the age of ten, the nurturing canine had helped raise more than thirty baby animals of all species, ranging from tiger cubs to pygmy hippos and even a porcupine. The Halls run Cango Wildlife Ranch, a popular tourist attraction in part because guests are able to interact with the animals, and they've noticed that Lisha steps right in whenever either of the Halls or a staffer shows up with an orphaned animal.

"If Lisha sees an animal being brought back in a box, she automatically assumes that it is to be cared for," said Nadine. "She would just walk up and lick the creature she was caring for."[1]

Though Lisha has never had a litter of her own, that hasn't dampened her motherly instincts. Indeed, even animal mothers who've had numerous litters sometimes hesitate to raise babies from another species. "They adjust more easily to her and when they see that she trusts us, they are more at ease around us,"[2] Nadine added.

118

Not only does Lisha help raise orphaned and abandoned baby animals that are brought in from outside the ranch, but she also helps out with those critters that are born at Cango but are abandoned by their mothers for a variety of reasons. Most of the baby animals born at the ranch have plenty of interaction with humans when only a few days old. If they have no maternal figure to guide them, they'll become a little too comfortable with humans, and indeed often start patterning their behavior after that of humans. They definitely need a little guidance from the animal world, and that's where Lisha comes in. She helps each baby retain their native animal instincts and teaches them how to act like an animal.

The Halls have had Lisha since she was a puppy, and they have never ceased to marvel at how the dog's maternal instincts kick in no matter the species, breed, or size. "We noticed early on that she didn't care if it was a cat or a porcupine," said Nadine. "She licks them and cares for them, almost like a mother would. Although, in the case of the porcupine, that was more amusing."[3]

Family Fact: The American Kennel Club selected the Labrador retriever as the most popular breed in the United States for more than twenty years in a row.

Family Fact: Ginger cats — also known as orange tabby cats — are much more likely to be male than female by about a four-to-one ratio.

The Ginger Tomcat and His Lion Cub

When Zara the lion cub was born to a lioness named Safina at the Linton Zoo in Cambridgeshire, Great Britain, in the spring of 2008, it was unclear whether the youngster would make it.

"We only hand-rear the cubs if it's absolutely necessary, but this was Safina's first baby and she couldn't feed her due to her young age and inexperience," said zoo director Kim Simmons, who assumed bottle-feeding responsibility for the young cub while her ginger tomcat, Arnie, took care of nuzzling, cuddling, and teaching Zara some household etiquette as well as instructing him in the ways of interacting with cats of another species.

Zara spent only six weeks with her surrogate feline father—going from a runty two pounds to ten pounds in that time—but both Arnie and Simmons were extremely reluctant to see the cub go. "Arnie loves having cubs in the house," said the zoo director. "As long as Zara's going to a good home with a good quality of life, I have to be happy, but I'll find it a struggle to part with her."[1]

Zara's new home is in Uganda, where she'll live at the Ugandan Wildlife Education Centre, a rehabilitation and conservation center in Entebbe where she should get along fine with felines of any species.

Family Fact: An Akita dog named Hachiko faithfully met his owner at the train station in Tokyo in the mid-1920s; when the man died, Hachiko returned to the train station to wait for his owner every day for nine years until he died in 1935.

The Akita and Her Lion Cub

In 1998 at the Glasgow Zoo in Scotland, zookeepers paired a full-grown Akita dog named Koneko with a tiny lion cub named Sam — the first Asiatic lion to be born in the zoo's sixty-year history — as a grand experiment. They'd read about sanctuaries and wildlife rehabilitation centers in Africa that had done this type of pairing as a matter of course, but they had yet to try what seemed like a daring and possibly dangerous technique at the time.

But like the other rescue groups, they also had experienced their fair share of seeing lion and tiger cubs that had been orphaned or abandoned or rejected by their mothers, and they were desperate for an alternative to bottle-feeding the cubs every two hours for weeks on end.

And so they decided to put an Akita — a Japanese dog known for its loyalty but that often possesses a wildly independent streak — to the test. They paired a female named Koneko — also known by her Anglicized name of Connie — with a lion cub named Sam in early 1998. It was a match made in heaven: The two bonded from the get-go.

A year later, the two were moved to the Dudley Zoo in England, and their close relationship continued to blossom. But it soon grew time for both to move off to greener pastures. Sam headed off to the Parken Zoo in Sweden where a matchmaker had fixed him up with Saria, an eighteen-month-old lioness, while Koneko was adopted by a family in England.

The Rabbit and Her Kittens

Since Melanie Humble worked at a veterinary hospital in Aberdeen, Scotland, she was well-accustomed to seeing all kinds of strays and unwanted animals cross the threshold of the office. She did her best to nurse them back to health and if necessary find good homes for them.

So when she agreed to foster a litter of five-week-old kittens that had been abandoned by their mother in the fall of 2007, she thought that her cat Ellie would enthusiastically help to care for the young ones. But as it turned out, her female rabbit Summer took over and helped to raise the kittens while Ellie basically ignored them.

Summer had originally been an outdoor rabbit, but Humble brought her into the house one night when a fireworks exhibition was scheduled nearby. That switch just so happened to coincide with her bringing the kittens home. Though she originally worried about how the rabbit would regard the kittens — and vice versa — as things turned out, it was perfect chemistry on both sides from the beginning, and the outdoor rabbit turned into an inside homebody and surrogate mother.

Humble assumed feeding responsibilities for the foster litter, giving them formula

through a syringe every few hours, which she admits is "a bit of a full-time job," while Summer the rabbit took over in the cuddling and nurturing department.

"They think she's their mum," said Humble. "She's a big fat rabbit and she just sits there quite happily and lets them climb all over her. It's lovely to see them all together."[1]

Family Fact: Rabbits that are kept as house pets can live up to twelve years.

The Pointer and Her Puma Cub

Ray Graham Jones ran a small wildlife park near Daventry, England. One night, a very young baby puma wandered away from its mother and ended up roaming around until morning calling out for help. Zoo staffers found the puma the next morning, and immediately returned it to his mother. Sadly, the mother repeatedly rebuffed the puma's attempts to get closer and nurse. Quite possibly the baby now smelled different and seemed unfamiliar after having gone astray.

Graham knew he had to act quickly. Infant cubs have to essentially nurse around the clock, and several hours had already passed since the puma last ate. The zookeeper quickly put together a suitable formula and tried to give it to the cub, but the baby refused to swallow the milk.

In desperation, Graham contacted a neighbor who happened to be a dog breeder. He knew there was a good chance there would be a nursing dog on the premises. Happily, there was indeed a pointer named Judy who had recently had a litter of pups, and so the zookeeper dashed over to the neighbor's house with the puma—by now christened Loopy—and nestled him in beside the puppies. If Judy minded, she didn't let on, and the dog accepted the baby puma into the fold without skipping a beat.

For his part, Loopy didn't appear to notice anything amiss, as he nuzzled his canine surrogate mom, played with his adopted siblings, and even started licking and caressing Judy just as if she was his real mother. After a few weeks of nursing, Graham gradually started to wean Loopy by feeding him a few handfuls of dog kibble at a time before making the move to a regular puma menu of meat and poultry. But Loopy's time with Judy had likely saved his life.

Family Fact: Pumas are also known as mountain lions, cougars, panthers, and catamounts.

The Pig and His Lamb

Edgar Alan Pig is the namesake of Edgar's Mission Farm Sancutary, a sixty-acre animal sanctuary in Victoria, Australia, with a unique specialty: Founder Pam Ahern concentrates on rescuing animals that would otherwise be headed for a dinner plate.

It all started with Edgar, a pig that Ahern bought from a piggery when actor James Cromwell—who played the farmer in the movie *Babe*—came to Victoria in 2003 and wanted to have a picture of himself taken with a pig to help alert people to the plight of farm animals, particularly pigs in factory farms. Ahern found a pig at a local farm, Cromwell posed with the pig, and Ahern planned the next day to find a sanctuary where Edgar—already named—could live out his natural life.

But when the next morning came, Ahern could no more send Edgar off to a sanctuary than she could send him back to the farm. And so she decided to start a rescue of her own devoted to taking in farm animals

Since then Edgar helped foster and serve as a surrogate father to a variety of different animals countless times in the seven years since he first arrived into Ahern's life. Plus, he became famous throughout Australia serving as a four-legged ambassador to draw attention to the issue; after all, it was the first time for many Australians that they had witnessed a pig walk on a leash, as Ahern gently led the pig out in public.

Edgar also served as a welcoming committee for the hundreds of orphaned and abandoned lambs, chickens, goats, and other barnyard animals that showed up at the sanctuary on a regular basis; around 250 live there at any one time. He had a particularly special relationship with a one-week-old lamb named Arnie, who he instantly took under his wing when Arnie first showed up at Edgar's Mission.

Edgar has proven that pigs do make great surrogate fathers—and mothers. And though Edgar passed away in 2010, his legacy still resonates in Australia and all over the world.

Family Fact: Pigs can be trained to sniff out truffles, an edible delicacy found in forests, as well a bombs and mines.

The Great Dane and
His Baby Chimp

Humans who decide to start a refuge for animals can face a great many challenges in a job that is, in reality, never-ending and requires twenty-four-hour attention. When Molly Badham and Nathalie Evans founded a sanctuary for monkeys and chimpanzees in Warwickshire, Great Britain, in 1963 they had little idea of the challenges they would face. Yet they carried on, and today it has grown into the internationally famous Twycross Zoo that boasts the largest zoo dedicated to primates in the world.

At the same time, they never would have guessed that one of the biggest contributors to their work to save infant and young chimps and monkeys would come in the form of a group of canines that served as everything from babysitters to playmates, and even surrogate mothers.

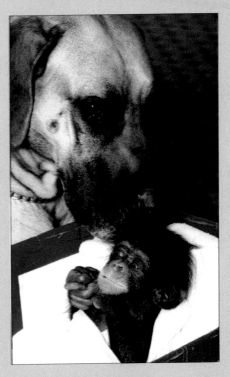

Though Badham and Evans called everything from French bulldogs to mutts into service, they particularly liked Great Danes for their gentle nature. "Great Danes showed the same caring attitude to all our orphans, and were incredibly tolerant when they were tormented and teased by the cheekier youngsters," said Molly Badham in her book *Molly's Zoo*.

One favorite dog was named Coaley — his previous owner delivered coal to houses — but when they first met, Badham almost opted for another dog because she thought he was too strong for them to manage, as he virtually dragged the rescue volunteer at the shelter down the path toward them. "When he came up to us and looked at us with his big, sad eyes, as if pleading for us to give him a chance, I relented. He was very thin and had obviously been fretting at the kennels."

Badham needn't have worried: Coaley turned out to be one of her best surrogate father canines. He took a particular shine to a tiny chimpanzee named Minnie. "We were bringing up chimps in the house, and Coaley adored them," said Badham. "He would let them wrestle with him, he'd chase around after them, and even when they teased him, he never took offense. He would let them get away with murder."[1]

Family Fact: Great Danes are one of the largest dog breeds around. Males can easily tip the scales at two hundred pounds and tower over their humans at six feet tall while standing on their hind legs.

The Tortoiseshell Cat
and Her Rottweiler Puppies

One day in Norfolk, Great Britain, in 2007, a cat named Sky gave birth to four kittens. Sky was a tortoiseshell, a feline mixed breed with a coat of patchy colors, most often brown, orange, black, and very little — if any — white. The tortoiseshell's owner, David Page, was an animal lover, and he made sure to check in on the mother cat and kittens several times a day to make sure everything was okay. A couple of days later, a Rottweiler named Roxy also

gave birth to six puppies on some property Page owned nearby. But unlike Sky, who had happily embraced motherhood, Roxy refused to nurse the puppies. Page believed that Roxy became stressed by the birth, and so he scooped up the puppies and brought them to his local veterinarian, who examined them and started them on a round of antibiotics.

Unfortunately, by the time Page had discovered them, they were in pretty bad shape, and two of the pups succumbed to pneumonia. He decided the only thing to do was to see if Sky would pitch in.

"I put the four, which were still alive at that stage in her box very gently, one by one alongside her kittens just to see what happened," he said. "They snuggled into her straight away."[1]

But then they started doing more than snuggling up to Sky for warmth: They actually started nursing, which the mother cat not only accepted but encouraged wholeheartedly.

"It's just amazing to think that Sky has taken so well to the puppies," said Page. "She has a lovely, gentle nature and treats them just like her kittens. They are just one big happy family."[2]

Family Fact: It's rare for a tortoiseshell cat to be a male.

Notes

INTRODUCTION

1. Alice Cooke, "Extraordinary Animal Friendships," *Country Life*, January 18, 2011.

2. "Gosling Who Thinks It's a Peacock," Rex Features, June 17, 2009.

3. Molly Badham, with Maureen Lawless, *Chimps with Everything: The Story of Twycross Zoo* (London: W. H. Allen, 1979), 112–13.

4. Molly Badham and Nathalie Evans, with Maureen Lawless, *Molly's Zoo: Monkey Mischief at Twycross* (London: Simon & Schuster UK, 2000), 200.

5. Susan Kauffmann, "Interspecies Friendships: When Cats Join the Pack," *Modern Dog Magazine*, Spring 2004.

6. Ibid.

THE GREYHOUND AND HER FAWN, HER FOX KITS, HER BUNNIES, AND . . .

1. Sian Powell, "Supermum! In the Past, Jasmine the Greyhound Has Fostered Birds, Rab-

bits and Fox Cubs . . . Her Latest Charge Is a Little Fawn Called Bramble," *Coventry Evening Telegraph*, July 16, 2008.

THE HEN AND HER DUCKLINGS

1. Nick Enoch, "Waddle We Look Like When We Grow Up, Mum? Hilda the Hen Hatches Clutch of Ducklings After Sitting on Wrong Nest," *Daily Mail*, April 4, 2012.

THE CAT AND HER SQUIRREL

1. "The Chanel Crossing: Perfume Spray Brings Together One Squirrel, Two Cats, and Ten Kittens," *Daily Mail*, September 14, 1996.

THE BOXER AND HIS KID

1. "Paternal Dog Billy Takes on an Unusual Kid," *Daily Mail*, February 28, 2008.

THE SPRINGER SPANIEL AND HER LAMBS

1. "Meet the Ultimate Sheepdog! Springer Spaniel Jess Rounds Up Orphaned Lambs and Feeds Them from a Bottle Herself," *Daily Mail*, September 18, 2012.

THE KELPIE AND HIS BABY CHICKS

1. "Dopey Dog Love Is Chick Magnet," Rex Features, May 28, 2010.

THE GOLDEN RETRIEVER AND HER BUNNIES

1. Tariq Tahir, "Cute Alert: Labrador Adopts Abandoned Baby Rabbits," *Metro*, May 24, 2011.

THE HEN AND HER FALCON CHICK

1. Kate Hurry, "Who Are You Calling Chicken? Tufty the Hen's Adopted Offspring Will Turn Out to Be a Bit of a Wild Thing," *Daily Mail*, April 24, 2001.

THE BORDER COLLIE AND HIS VIETNAMESE POT-BELLIED PIGLETS

1. "Mac the Maternal Border Collie Foster Dog Who Stepped into the Breach," Rex Features, April 25, 1997.

THE REED WARBLER AND HER CUCKOO CHICK

1. "Cuckolded! The Little Red Warblers Fooled into Feeding Cuckoo Chick Three Times Their Size," *Daily Mail*, June 24, 2011.

THE GERMAN SHEPHERD AND HER KITTENS

1. Donna Carton, "A Kitten's Best Friend in Frankston," *Frankston Standard Leader*, February 23, 2009.

THE OWL AND HER GOSLING

1. James Tait, "Owl Be There for You," *Mirror* (London), May 31, 2004.

THE GOAT AND HER WOLF PUP

1. "Wolf and Goat Become Inseparable, Nanyuanzi Village, China," Rex USA, June 17, 2010.

THE CHICKEN, THE GOOSE, AND THEIR THREE DUCKLINGS

1. "Henrietta's Farmyard Family, Thayer, Iowa, America," Rex USA, November 2009.

THE GERMAN SHORTHAIRED POINTER AND HER OWLET

1. "Cherub the Baby Owl Is Reared with a Little Help from Pointer Kiera at the Devon Bird of Prey Centre in Newton Abbot, Devon, Britain," Rex USA, May 13, 2009.

THE TAMARIN MONKEY AND HIS TWIN BABY MARMOSETS

1. "Tom the Monkey Childminder," Rex Features, May 17, 2011.

THE POINTER MIX AND HIS JOEY

1. "Best Mates, the Baby Kangaroo, and the Wonder Dog That Saved It," *Daily Mail*, March 31, 2008.

THE GREAT DANE AND HIS FAWN

1. "They Say Every Dog Has Its Doe," *Sun*, May 6, 2008.
2. "Great Dane Makes a Deer Friend," *Telegraph*, May 6, 2008.

THE GERMAN SHEPHERD DOBERMAN MIX AND HIS BABY BADGER

1. "A Badger's Best Friend," *Daily Mail*, April 6, 1998.

THE BORDER COLLIE AND HIS HYENA AND TIGER CUBS

1. Suzannah Hills, "Puppy Love: But How Long Will It Last?" *Daily Mail*, May 14, 2012.

THE LIONESS AND THE ANTELOPE CALF

1. Emma Reynolds, "Extraordinary Moment Wounded Lioness Shows Softer Side by Adopting Baby Antelope," *Daily Mail*, October 8, 2012.

THE FOXHOUND AND HER FOX KITS

1. David Hennessey, "Rescue Dog Nurses Baby Foxes," *Greenwich Time*, September 22, 2011.

THE DALMATIAN AND HER LAMB

1. Mark Molloy, "Loving Dalmatian Adopts Abandoned 'Sheep in Dog's Clothing,'" *Metro*, August 15, 2012.

THE BOXER AND HER PIGLET

1. Paul Milligan, "A Piglet's Best Friend: Animal Forms Unbreakable Bond with Boxer Dog After Being Orphaned at One Day Old," *Daily Mail*, April 30, 2012.

2. Rachael Misstear, "Unlikely Friendship of Norfolk Piggy and Welsh Puggy Is a YouTube Hit: Boxer Saved from Welsh Puppy Farm Hams It Up," *Western Mail*, December 24, 2011.

THE FOX AND HER KITTENS

1. John Drysdale, e-mail correspondence with author, December 7, 2012.

THE GERMAN SHEPHERD AND HER BENGAL TIGER CUBS

1. "Tiger," Reuters, April 2, 2001.
2. Holly Barnes, "Puppy Love: Vet Robert Zammit's Dog, Pepper, Administers TLC to One of the Orphaned Tiger Cubs Yesterday," *Sun-Herald*, January 4, 2001.

THE ORANGUTAN AND HIS LION CUBS

1. Paul Bentley, "I've Got My Hands Full Aping Mum: Orangutan Cradles Lion Cubs in Unlikely Babysitter Role," *Daily Mail*, September 3, 2010.

THE BABOON AND HER BUSH BABY

1. Sahra Abdi, "Clinging to the Underbelly of a Baboon, Gakii, a Three-Month-Old Orphaned Bush Baby, Has Plumped for an Unlikely Surrogate Mother," Reuters, June 10, 2011.

THE YELLOW LAB AND HIS DUCKLING

1. "The Dog and the Duck: Labrador 'Adopts' Bird Whose Mother Was Killed By a Fox," *Daily Mail*, April 3, 2012.

THE CHICKEN AND HER ROTTWEILER PUPPIES

1. Heidi Blake, "Hen That Thinks It's a Dog Takes Litter of Puppies Under Its Wing," *Telegraph*, March 4, 2010.

THE PEACOCK AND HER GOSLING

1. "Gosling Who Thinks It's a Peacock," Rex Features, June 17, 2009.

THE LABRADOR AND HER BABY PYGMY HIPPO, HER TIGER CUBS, HER PORCUPINE, AND . . .

1. "Motherly Love: Lisha the Labrador Plays Surrogate to . . . Tigers, Cheetahs, Porcupines, and Even a Pygmy Hippo," *Daily Mail*, February 2, 2009.
2. Marelize Potgieter, "Lisha Helps Raise Baby Tigers," *Die Hoorn*, February 12, 2009.
3. "Motherly Love," *Daily Mail*, February 2, 2009.

THE GINGER TOMCAT AND HIS LION CUB

1. Chris Johnson, "Zara the Lion Cub and Arnie the House Cat Make a Purrfect Couple," *Daily Mail*, July 7, 2008.

THE RABBIT AND HER KITTENS

1. "Having Kittens: Rabbit Adopts New Feline Family," *Daily Mail*, November 19, 2007.

THE GREAT DANE AND HIS BABY CHIMP

1. Badham, *Molly's Zoo*, 201–2.

THE TORTOISESHELL CAT AND HER ROTTWEILER PUPPIES

1. "Cat Adopts Rottweiler Puppies," *Mumbai Mirror*, July 9, 2007.
2. "Rottweiler Pup Whose Mum's a Moggy," *Daily Mail*, July 6, 2007.

Photo Credits

The Greyhound and Her Fawn, Her Fox Kits, Her Bunnies, and . . . : Geoff Grewcock

The Hen and Her Ducklings: Bournemouth News/Rex Features

The Cat and Her Squirrel: Nils Jorgensen/Rex USA

The Boxer and His Kid: Richard Austin/Rex USA

The Springer Spaniel and Her Lambs: Richard Austin/Rex USA

The Kelpie and His Baby Chicks: Nicholas Welsh/Newspix/Rex/Rex USA

The Golden Retriever and Her Bunnies: Tina Case/Rex Features

The Cat and Her Ducklings: Masatoshi Okauchi/Rex USA

The Hen and Her Falcon Chick: Julian Hamilton/Rex USA

The Border Collie and His Vietnamese Pot-Bellied Piglets: Mike Hollist/Daily Mail/Rex USA

The Reed Warbler and Her Cuckoo Chick: Solent News/Rex/Rex USA

The German Shepherd and Her Kittens: Newspix/Rex Features Ltd.

The Owl and Her Gosling: Kenny Elrick/Rex USA

The Goat and Her Wolf Pup: Quirky China/Rex Features Ltd.

The Chicken, the Goose, and Their Three Ducklings: Karine Aigner/Rex/Rex USA

The German Shorthaired Pointer and Her Owlet: Richard Austin/Rex USA

The Tamarin Monkey and His Twin Baby Marmosets: Jeremy Durkin/Rex Features

The Pointer Mix and His Joey: Newspix / Rex USA

The Great Dane and His Fawn: Richard Austin/Rex USA

The German Shepherd Doberman Mix and His Baby Badger: Richard Austin/Rex USA

The Border Collie and His Hyena and Tiger Cubs: Gallo Images/Rex/Rex USA

The Lioness and the Antelope Calf: Adri de Visser/Caters News

The Foxhound and Her Fox Kits: Helen Neafsey, Hearst Connecticut Media Group

The Cow and Her Lambs: Stephen Barker/Rex USA

The Dog and His Baby Monkey: Top Photo Group/Rex USA

The Dalmatian and Her Lamb: Media Mode Pty Ltd/Rex/Rex USA

The Cat and Her Baby Chicks: Reuters/Ali Jarekji

The Mutt and Her Bush Baby: John Drysdale

The Airedale Terrier and Her Guinea Pigs: Elaine Hu

The Sow and Her Kitten: John Drysdale

The Pointer Rhodesian Ridgeback Mix and Her Baby Llama: John Drysdale

The Boxer and Her Piglet: Maurice Gray/Caters News

The Chimpanzee and Her Puppies: John Drysdale

The Fox and Her Kittens: John Drysdale

The German Shepherd and Her Bengal Tiger Cubs: Paul Lovelace/Rex USA

The Bulldog and Her Baby Squirrels: John Drysdale

The Orangutan and His Lion Cubs: Splash News

The Baboon and Her Bush Baby: Reuters/Thomas Mukoya

The Yellow Lab and His Duckling: SWNS

The Chicken and Her Rottweiler Puppies: Adam Harnett/Caters

The Chihuahua and His Baby Marmoset: John Drysdale

The Peacock and Her Gosling: Rex USA

The Labrador and Her Baby Pygmy Hippo, Her Tiger Cubs, Her Porcupine and . . . : Courtesy of Cango Wildlife Ranch, Oudtshoorn, South Africa, and the Hall Family in loving memory of Lisha

The Ginger Tomcat and His Lion Cub: SWNS

The Akita and Her Lion Cub: Mike Hollist/Daily Mail/Rex/Rex USA

The Rabbit and Her Kittens: Northscot Press Agency/Rex USA

The Pointer and Her Puma Cub: John Drysdale

The Pig and His Lamb: Alex Coppel/Newspix/Rex/Rex USA

The Great Dane and His Baby Chimp: Mike Hollist/Associated Newspapers/Rex/Rex USA

The Tortoiseshell Cat and Her Rottweiler Puppies: Jerry Daws/Rex USA

Acknowledgments

Eternal thanks to Superagent, aka Scott Mendel.

Followed by Peter Joseph at Thomas Dunne Books, an imprint of St. Martin's Press, as well as Tom Dunne, Sally Richardson, and Matthew Shear for launching this whole canine/critter trajectory with *Dogs of War* and following up with *Dogs of Courage*. A special shout-out to Margaret Sutherland Brown and her successor, Melanie Fried, for possessing the unique talent to keep track of my whereabouts, a science that often confuses even me. Also to Joan Higgins for being the consummate publicist when it comes to anything involving critter books.

On to the buddies in various geographic corners who provide me and my laptop a place for me to land every so often:

In New Hampshire, thanks to Cheryl Trotta, who helps me keep my life somewhat organized in exchange for massive amounts of brisket, chocolaty things, and decent Chianti, and Sam Trotta, to whom I will be forever known as Good Mommy, and a grudging admiration for the stubbornness of Cosmo, aka GETOUTTATHEKITCHEN; Dean Hollatz and Leslie Caputo, who I think at this point just shake their heads with pity at my luggage explosions and last-minute appearances for which I pay a required toll in the form of See's Toffee-ettes; and, of course, Bob and Reagan Poochie DiPrete.

In Charleston, thanks to John Willson and David Porter for making Monday nights so fortifying that I can then proceed to effortlessly slog my way through the rest of the week chained to the computer. Also to Michael Murray whenever he happens to land there.

Finally, thanks to Alex Ishii, for being good for something . . .